PEPPER & SALT OR, SEASONING FOR YOUNG FOLK

PEPPER & SALT OR, SEASONING FOR YOUNG FOLK

Howard Pyle

www.General-Books.net

Publication Data:

Title: Pepper Salt Or, Seasoning for Young Folk
Author: Pyle, Howard, 1853-1911
Reprinted: 2010, General Books, Memphis, Tennessee, USA

1

PEPPER & SALT OR, SEASONING FOR YOUNG FOLK

Pepper Salt,

or

Seasoning for *Young Folk*
Prepared by
Howard Pyle
THIS SPECIAL EDITION IS PUBLISHED BY ARRANGEMENT WITH THE
PUBLISHERS OF THE REGULAR EDITION
HARPER BROTHERS
BY
E.M. HALE AND COMPANY
EAU CLAIRE, WISCONSIN
title page

Preface
Here, my little man, you may hold my cap and bells,–and you, over there, may hold the bauble! Now, then, I am ready to talk as a wise man should and am a giddy-pated jester no longer!

This is what I have to say:

One must have a little pinch of seasoning in this dull, heavy life of ours; one should never look to have all the troubles, the labors, and the cares, with never a whit of innocent jollity and mirth. Yes, one must smile now and then, if for nothing else than to lift the corners of the lips in laughter that are only too often dragged down in sorrow.

It is for this that I sit here now, telling you all manner of odd quips and jests until yon sober, wise man shakes his head and goes his way, thinking that I am even more of a shallow-witted knave than I really am. But, prut! Who cares for that? I am sure that I do not if you do not.

Yet listen! One must not look to have nothing but pepper and salt in this life of ours–no, indeed! At that rate we would be worse off than we are now. I only mean that it is a good and pleasant thing to have something to lend the more solid part a little savor now and then!

So, here I'll sit; and, perhaps, when you have been good children, and have learned your lessons or done your work, your mother will let you come and play a little while with me. I will always be ready and waiting for you here, and I will warrant your mother that I will do you no harm with anything that I may tell you. If I can only make you laugh and be merry for a little while, then my work will be well done, and I will be glad in the doing of it.

And now give me my cap and bells again, for my wits are growing cold without them; and you will be pleased to reach me my bauble once more, for I love to have him by me.

Will you be seated? And you, over there, seat the baby on the grass! Are you ready? Very well; then I will tell you a story, and it shall be about "The Skillful Huntsman."

preface decoration

Table of Contents

     table of contents decoration

PEPPER AND SALT

The Skillful Huntsman

Once upon a time there was a lad named Jacob Boehm, who was a practical huntsman.

One day Jacob said to his mother, "Mother, I would like to marry Gretchen–the nice, pretty little daughter of the Herr Mayor."

Jacob's mother thought that he was crazy. "Marry the daughter of the Herr Mayor, indeed! You want to marry the daughter of the Herr Mayor? Listen; many a man wants and wants, and nothing comes of it!"

That was what Jacob Boehm's mother said to him.

But Jacob was deaf in that ear; nothing would do but his mother must go to the Herr Mayor, and ask for leave for him to marry Gretchen. And Jacob begged and begged so prettily that at last his mother promised to go and do as he wished. So off she went, though doubt was heavy in her shoes, for she did not know how the Herr Mayor would take it.

"So Jacob wants to marry Gretchen, does he?" said the Herr Mayor.

Yes; that was what Jacob wanted.

"And is he a practical huntsman?" said the Herr Mayor.

Oh yes, he was that.

"So good," said the Herr Mayor. "Then tell Jacob that when he is such a clever huntsman as to be able to shoot the whiskers off from a running hare without touching the skin, then he can have Gretchen."

Jacob's Mother The Herr Mayor "Jacob's Mother The Herr Mayor"

Then Jacob's mother went back home again. "Now," said she, "Jacob will, at least, be satisfied."

"Yes," said Jacob, when she had told him all that the Herr Mayor had said to her, "that is a hard thing to do; but what one man has done, another man can." So he shouldered his gun, and started away into the world to learn to be as clever a huntsman as the Herr Mayor had said.

He plodded on and on until at last he fell in with a tall stranger dressed all in red.

"Where are you going, Jacob?" said the tall stranger, calling him by his name, just as if he had eaten pottage out of the same dish with him.

"I am going," said Jacob, "to learn to be so clever a huntsman that I can shoot the whiskers off from a running hare without touching the skin."

"That is a hard thing to learn," said the tall stranger.

Yes; Jacob knew that it was a hard thing; but what one man had done another man could do.

"What will you give me if I teach you to be as clever a huntsman as that?" said the tall stranger.

"What will you take to teach me?" said Jacob; for he saw that the stranger had a horse's hoof instead of a foot, and he did not like his looks, I can tell you.

"Oh, it is nothing much that I want," said the tall man; "only just sign your name to this paper–that is all."

But what was in the paper? Yes; Jacob had to know what was in the paper before he would set so much as a finger to it.

Oh, there was nothing in the paper, only this: that when the red one should come for Jacob at the end of ten years' time, Jacob should promise to go along with him whithersoever he should take him.

At this Jacob hemmed and hawed and scratched his head, for he did not know about that. "All the same," said he, "I will sign the paper, but on one condition."

Jacob and The Red One "Jacob and The Red One"

At this the red one screwed up his face as though he had sour beer in his mouth, for he did not like the sound of the word "condition." "Well," said he, "what is the condition?"

"It is only this," said Jacob: "that you shall be *my* servant for the ten years, and if, in all that time, I should chance to ask you a question that you cannot answer, then I am to be my own man again."

Oh, if that was all, the red man was quite willing for that.

Then he took Jacob's gun, and blew down into the barrel of it. "Now," said he, "you are as skillful a huntsman as you asked to be."

"That I must try," said Jacob. So Jacob and the red one went around hunting here and hunting there until they scared up a hare. "Shoot!" said the red one; and Jacob shot. Clip! off flew the whiskers of the hare as neatly as one could cut them off with the barber's shears.

"Yes, good!" said Jacob, "now I am a skillful huntsman."

Then the stranger in red gave Jacob a little bone whistle, and told him to blow in it whenever he should want him. After that Jacob signed the paper, and the stranger went one way and he went home again.

Well, Jacob brushed the straws off from his coat, and put a fine shine on his boots, and then he set off to the Herr Mayor's house.

"How do you find yourself, Jacob?" said the Herr Mayor.

"So good," said Jacob.

"And are you a skillful huntsman now?" said the Herr Mayor.

Oh yes, Jacob was a skillful huntsman now.

Yes, good! But the Herr Mayor must have proof of that. Now, could Jacob shoot a feather out of the tail of the magpie flying over the trees yonder?

Oh yes! nothing easier than that. So Jacob raised the gun to his cheek. Bang! went the gun, and down fell a feather from the tail of the magpie. At this the Herr Mayor stared and stared, for he had never seen such shooting.

"And now may I marry Gretchen?" said Jacob.

Jacob shoots at the Magpie "Jacob shoots at the Magpie"

At this the Herr Mayor scratched his head, and hemmed and hawed. No; Jacob could not marry Gretchen yet, for he had always said and sworn that the man who should marry Gretchen should bring with him a plough that could go of itself, and plough three furrows at once. If Jacob would show him such a plough as that, then he might marry Gretchen and welcome. That was what the Herr Mayor said.

Jacob did not know how about that; perhaps he could get such a plough, perhaps he could not. If such a plough was to be had, though, he would have it. So off he went home again, and the Herr Mayor thought that he was rid of him now for sure and certain.

But when Jacob had come home, he went back of the woodpile and blew a turn or two on the little bone whistle that the red stranger had given him. No sooner had he done this than the other stood before him as suddenly as though he had just stepped out of the door of nowheres.

"What do you want, Jacob?" said he.

"I would like," said Jacob, "to have a plough that can go by itself and plough three furrows at once."

"That you shall have," said the red one. Then he thrust his hand into his breeches pocket, and drew forth the prettiest little plough that you ever saw. He stood it on the ground before Jacob, and it grew large as you see it in the picture. "Plough away," said he, and then he went back again whither he had come.

So Jacob laid his hands to the plough and–whisk!–away it went like John Stormwetter's colt, with Jacob behind it. Out of the farm-yard they went, and down the road, and so to the Herr Mayor's house, and behind them lay three fine brown furrows, smoking in the sun.

When the Herr Mayor saw them coming he opened his eyes, you may be sure, for he had never seen such a plough as that in all of his life before.

"And now," said Jacob, "I should like to marry Gretchen, if you please."

At this the Herr Mayor hemmed and hawed and scratched his head again. No; Jacob could not marry Gretchen yet, for the Herr Mayor had always said and sworn that the man who married Gretchen should bring with him a purse that always had two pennies in it and could never be emptied, no matter how much was taken out of it.

Jacob and the Magic Plough "Jacob and the Magic Plough"

Jacob did not know how about that; perhaps he could get it and perhaps he could not. If such a thing was to be had, though, he would have it, as sure as the Mecklenburg folks brew sour beer. So off he went home again, and the Herr Mayor thought that now he was rid of him for certain.

But Jacob went back of the woodpile and blew on his bone whistle again, and once more the red one came at his bidding.

"What will you have now?" said he to Jacob.

"I should like," said Jacob, "to have a purse which shall always have two pennies in it, no matter how much I take out of it."

"That you shall have," said the red one; whereupon he thrust his hand into his pocket, and fetched out a beautiful silken purse with two pennies in it. He gave the purse to Jacob, and then he went away again as quickly as he had come.

After he had gone, Jacob began taking pennies out of his purse and pennies out of his purse, until he had more than a hatful—hui! I would like to have such a purse as that.

Then he marched off to the Herr Mayor's house with his chin up, for he might hold his head as high as any, now that he had such a purse as that in his pocket. As for the Herr Mayor, he thought that it was a nice, pretty little purse; but could it do this and that as he had said?

Jacob would show him that; so he began taking pennies and pennies out of it, until he had filled all the pots and pans in the house with them. And now might he marry Gretchen?

Yes; that he might! So said the Herr Mayor; for who would not like to have a lad for a son-in-law who always had two pennies more in his purse than he could spend.

So Jacob married his Gretchen, and, between his plough and his purse, he was busy enough, I can tell you.

So the days went on and on and on until the ten years had gone by and the time had come for the red one to fetch Jacob away with him. As for Jacob, he was in a sorry state of dumps, as you may well believe.

At last Gretchen spoke to him. "See, Jacob," said she, "what makes you so down in the mouth?"

"Oh! nothing at all," said Jacob.

But this did not satisfy Gretchen, for she could see that there was more to be told than Jacob had spoken. So she teased and teased, until at last Jacob told her all, and that the red one was to come the next day and take him off as his servant, unless he could ask him a question which he could not answer.

"Prut!" said Gretchen, "and is that all? Then there is no stuffing to that sausage, for I can help you out of your trouble easily enough." Then she told Jacob that when the next day should come he should do thus and so, and she would do this and that, and between them they might cheat the red one after all.

So, when the next day came, Gretchen went into the pantry and smeared herself all over with honey. Then she ripped open a bed and rolled herself in the feathers.

By-and-by came the red one. Rap! tap! tap! he knocked at the door.

"Are you ready to go with me now, Jacob?" said he.

Yes; Jacob was quite ready to go, only he would like to have one favor granted him first.

"What is it that you want?" said the red one.

"Only this," said Jacob: "I would like to shoot one more shot out of my old gun before I go with you."

Oh, if that was all, he might do that and welcome. So Jacob took down his gun, and he and the red one went out together, walking side by side, for all the world as though they were born brothers.

Jacob and the Red One go hunting together "Jacob and the Red One go hunting together"

By-and-by they saw a wren. "Shoot at that," said the red one.

"Oh no," said Jacob, "that is too small."

So they went on a little farther.

By-and-by they saw a raven. "Shoot at that, then," said the red one.

"Oh no," said Jacob, "that is too black."

So they went on a little farther.

By-and-by they came to a ploughed field, and there was something skipping over the furrows that looked for all the world like a great bird. That was Gretchen; for the feathers stuck to the honey and all over her, so that she looked just like a great bird.

"Shoot at that! shoot at that!" said the red one, clapping his hands together.

"Oh yes," said Jacob, "I will shoot at that." So he raised his gun and took aim. Then he lowered his gun again. "But what is it?" said he.

At this the red one screwed up his eyes, and looked and looked, but for the life of him he could not tell what it was.

"No matter what it is," said he, "only shoot and be done with it, for I must be going."

"Yes, good! But what *is* it?" said Jacob.

Then the red one looked and looked again, but he could tell no better this time than he could before. "It may be this and it may be that," said he. "Only shoot and be done with it, for they are waiting for me at home."

"Yes, my friend," said Jacob, "that is all very good; only tell me what it is and I will shoot."

"Thunder and lightning!" bawled the red one, *"I do not know what it is!"*

"Then be off with you!" said Jacob, "for, since you cannot answer my question, all is over between us two."

At this the red one had to leave Jacob, so he fled away over hill and dale, bellowing like a bull.

As for Jacob and Gretchen, they went back home together, very well pleased with each other and themselves.

And the meaning of all this is, that many another
man beside Jacob Boehm would find himself
in a pretty scrape only for his wife.

Jacob and Gretchen get the best of the Red One and go home together happily.
"Jacob and Gretchen get the best of the Red One and go home together happily."

This is a full page illustrated poem depicting the magpie in the poem, with the
poem weaving through the pictures.

TWO OPINIONS

(Ye first opinion)
A noisy chattering Magpie once
A talking gabbling hairbrained dunce
Came by where a sign-post stood.
He nodded his head with a modish air
And said "good day" for he wasn't aware
That the sign-post pointing its finger there
Was only a block of wood.
Quoth he, "An exceedingly sultry day.
T'is more like June than the first of May."
The post said never a word.
"I've just dropped over from Lincolnshire.
My home is in the Cathedral Spire–
The air is cooler and purer the higher
You get–as you've doubtless heard."
So on he chattered with never a stop,
And on and on till you'd think he would drop.
(The post was dumb as your hat.)
But so as the pie could say his say
He didn't care whether it spoke all day;
For thus he observed as he walked away–
"An intelligent creature that."
(Ye second opinion)
Now once when the sky was pouring rain,
The Magpie chanced to come by again–
And there stood the post in the wet.
"Helloa." said the Magpie. "What you here
Pray tell me I beg is there sheltering near–
A terrible day for this time of the year.
T'would make a Saint Anthony fret."
"I beg your pardon–I didn't quite hear."
(Then louder) "I say is there sheltering near"
But the post was as dumb as Death.
"What can't you answer a question pray
You will not–No–Then I'll say good-day."
And flirting his tail he walked away.
"You'r a fool." (this under his breath.)

L'ENVOY
The moral that this story traces
Is–Circumstances alter cases.
Howard Pyle

This is an illustrated poem, with the top half being an old woman going up then down a hill. The bottom is the poem, with court jesters on either side, left side titled Hope in Adversity, right titled Fear in Prosperity.

Ye song of ye foolish old woman.

I saw an old woman go up a steep hill,
And she chuckled and laughed, as she went, with a will.
And yet, as she went,
Her body was bent,
With a load as heavy as sins in Lent.
"Oh! why do you chuckle, old woman;" says I,
"As you climb up the hill-side so steep and so high?"
"Because, don't you see,
I'll presently be,
At the top of the hill. He! he!" says she.
I saw the old woman go downward again;
And she easily travelled, with never a pain;
Yet she loudly cried,
And gustily sighed,
And groaned, though the road was level and wide.
"Oh! why, my old woman," says I, "do you weep,
When you laughed, as you climbed up the hill-side so steep?"
"High-ho! I am vexed,
Because I expects,"
Says she, "I shall ache in climbing the next."
H. Pyle

This is a full page illustrated poem depicting the geese acting out the poem.

A NEWSPAPER PUFF

Twelve geese
In a row
(So these
Always go).
Down-hill
They meander,
Tail to bill;
First the gander.
So they stalked,
Bold as brass
As they walked
To the grass.
Suddenly
Stopped the throng;

Plain to see
Something's wrong
Yes; there is
Something white!
No quiz;
Clear to sight.
('Twill amuse
When you're told
'Twas a news-
Paper old.)
Gander spoke.
Braver bird
Never broke
Egg, I've heard:
"Stand here
Steadily,
Never fear,
Wait for me."
Forth he went,
Cautious, slow,
Body bent,
Head low.
All the rest
Stood fast,
Waiting for
What passed.
Wind came
With a caper,
Caught same
Daily paper.
Up it sailed
In the air;
Courage failed
Then and there.
Scared well
Out of wits;
Nearly fell
Into fits.
Off they sped,
Helter-skelter,
'Till they'd fled
Under shelter.
Poor geese!
Never mind;
Other geese

One can find,
Cut the same
Foolish caper
At empty wind
In a paper.
H. Pyle

This is a full page illustrated poem, depicting: the three as they start the journey, the shoemaker with his lady, the tailor and baker on the path, the tailor lounging in the Inn, and the baker wandering "To Nowhere."

THREE FORTUNES

A merry young shoemaker,
And a tailor, and a baker,
    Went to seek their fortunes, for they had been told,
Where a rainbow touched the ground,
(If it only could be found,)
Was a purse that should be always full of gold.
So they traveled day by day,
In a jolly, jocund way
Till the shoemaker a pretty lass espied;
When quoth he, "It seems to me,
There can never, never be,
Better luck than this in all the world beside."
So the others said good-bye,
And went on, till by-and-by
They espied a shady inn beside the way;
Where the Hostess fair,–a widow–
In a lone seclusion hid; "Oh,
Here is luck!" the tailor said, "and here I'll stay."
So the baker jogged along,
All alone, with ne'er a song,
Or a jest; and nothing tempted him to stay.
But he went from bad to worse,
For he never found the purse,
And for all I know he is wandering to this day.
It is better, on the whole,
For an ordinary soul,
(So I gather from this song I've tried to sing,)
For to take the luck that may
Chance to fall within his way,
Than to toil for an imaginary thing.
H. Pyle

CLAUS HIS WONDERFUL STAFF

Hans and Claus were born brothers. Hans was the elder and Claus was the younger; Hans was the richer and Claus was the poorer–that is the way that the world goes sometimes.

Everything was easy for Hans at home; he drank much beer, and had sausages and white bread three times a day; but Claus worked and worked, and no luck came of it–that, also, is the way that the world goes sometimes.

One time Claus spoke to Hans of this matter. "See, Hans," said he, "you should give me some money, for that which belongs to one brother should help the other."

But Hans saw through different colored spectacles than Claus. No; he would do nothing of the kind. If Claus wanted money he had better go out into, the world to look for it; for some folks said that money was rolling about in the wide world like peas on a threshing-floor. So said Hans, for Claus was so poor that Hans was ashamed of him, and wanted him to leave home so as to be rid of him for good and all.

This was how Claus came to go out into the world.

But before he went, he cut himself a good stout staff of hazel-wood to help his heavy feet over the road.

Now the staff that Claus had cut was a rod of witch-hazel, which has the power of showing wherever treasure lies buried. But Claus knew no more of that than the chick in the shell.

So off he went into the world, walking along with great contentment, kicking up little clouds of dust at every step, and whistling as gayly as though trouble had never been hatched from mares' eggs. By-and-by he came to the great town, and then he went to the market-place and stood, with many others, with a straw in his mouth–for that meant that he wanted to take service with somebody.

Presently there came along an old, old man, bent almost double with the weight of the years which he carried upon his shoulders. This was a famous doctor of the black-arts. He had read as many as a hundred books, so that he was more learned than any man in all of the world–even the minister of the village. He knew, as well as the birds know when the cherries are ripe, that Claus had a stick of witch-hazel, so he came to the market-place, peering here and peering there, just as honest folks do when they are looking for a servant. After a while he came to where Claus was, and then he stopped in front of him. "Do you want to take service, my friend?" said he.

Yes, that was what Claus wanted; why else should he stand in the market-place with a straw in his mouth?

Well, they bargained and bargained, and talked and talked, and the end of the matter was that Claus agreed to sell his services to the old master of black-arts for seven pennies a week. So they made their bargain, and off went the master with Claus at his heels. After they had come a little distance away from the crowd at the marketplace, the master of black-arts asked Claus where he had got that fine staff of hazel.

Claus and the Master of Black-Arts "Claus and the Master of Black-Arts"

"Oh, I got it over yonder," said Claus, pointing with his thumb.

But could he find the place again?

Well, Claus did not know how about that; perhaps he could, and perhaps he could not.

But suppose that Claus had a thaler in his hand, *then* could he find the place again?

Oh yes; in that case Claus was almost sure that he could find the place again.

So good. Then here was a bottle of yellow water. If Claus would take the bottle of yellow water, and pour it over the stump from which he had cut his staff, there would come seven green snakes out of a hole at the foot of the hazel-bush. After these seven snakes, there would come a white snake, with a golden crown on its head, from out of the same hole. Now if Claus would catch that white snake in the empty bottle, and bring it to the master of black-arts, he should have not one thaler, but two—that was what the master said.

Oh yes, Claus could do that; that was no such hard thing. So he took the bottle of yellow water and off he went.

By-and-by he came to the place where he had cut his hazel-twig. There he did as the master of black-arts had told him; he poured the yellow water over the stump of hazel from which he had cut his staff. Then everything happened just as the other had said: first there came seven green snakes out of the hole at the foot of the hazel-bush, and after they had all gone, there came a white snake, with a little golden crown on its head, and with its body gleaming like real silver. Then Claus caught the white snake, and put it into the bottle and corked it up tightly. After he had done this he went back to the master of black-arts again.

Now this white snake was what the folk call a tomtsnake in that land. Whoever eats of a broth made of it can understand the language of all the birds of the air and all the beasts of the field; so nobody need wonder that the master was as glad as glad could be to have his white snake safe and sound.

Claus and the White Snake "Claus and the White Snake"

He bade Claus build a fire of dry wood, and as soon as there was a good blaze he set a pot of water upon it to boil. When the water in the pot began to boil, he chopped up the white snake into little pieces and threw them into it. So the snake boiled and boiled and boiled, and Claus stared with wonder as though he would never shut his eyes again.

Now it happened that just about the time that the broth was cooked, the master was called out of the room for this or for that. No sooner was his back turned than Claus began to wonder what the broth was like. "I will just have a little taste," said he to himself; "surely it can do no harm to the rest of the soup." So he stuck his finger first into the broth and then into his mouth; but what the broth tasted like he never could tell, for just then the master came in again, and Claus was so frightened at what he had done that he had no wits to think of the taste of anything.

Presently the master of black-arts went to the pot of broth, and, taking off the lid, began smelling of it. But no sooner had he sniffed a smell of the steam than he began thumping his head with his knuckles, and tearing his hair, and stamping his feet. "*Somebody's had a finger in my broth!!!*" he roared. For the master knew at once that all the magic had been taken out of it by the touch of Claus's finger.

As for poor Claus, he was so frightened that he fell upon his knees, and began begging: "Oh! dear master—" But he got no further than this, for the master bawled at him,

"You have taken the best,
You may have the rest."

And so saying, he threw pot and broth and all at Claus, so that if he hadn't ducked his head he might have been scalded to death. Then Claus ran out into the street, for he saw that there was no place for him to stay in that house.

Now in the street there was a cock and a hen, scratching and clucking together in the dust, and Claus understood every word that they said to each other, so he stopped and listened to them.

This is what they said:

The cock said to the hen, "Yonder goes our new serving-man."

And the hen said to the cock, "Yes, yonder he goes."

And the cock said to the hen, "He is leaving the best behind him."

THE MASTER IS ANGRY "THE MASTER IS ANGRY"

And the hen said to the cock, "What is it that he is leaving?"

And the cock said to the hen, "He is leaving behind him the witch-hazel staff that he brought with him."

And the hen said to the cock, "Yes, that is so. He would be a fool to leave that behind, yet he is not the first one to think that peas are pebbles."

As for Claus, you can guess how he opened his eyes, for he saw how the land lay, and that he had other ears than he had before.

"Hui!" said he, "that is good! I have bought more for my penny than I had in my bargain."

As for the hazel staff, he was not going to leave that behind, you may be sure. So he sneaked about the place till he laid hand on it again; then he stepped away, right foot foremost, for he did not know what the master of black-arts might do to him if he should catch him.

Well, after he had left the town, he went along, tramp! tramp! tramp! until, by-and-by, he grew tired and sat down beneath an oak-tree to rest himself.

Claus listens to the talk of the two ravens "Claus listens to the talk of the two ravens"

Now, as he sat there, looking up through the leaves, thinking of nothing at all, two ravens came flying and lit in the tree above him. After a while the ravens began talking together, and this was what they said:

The one raven said, "Yonder is poor Claus sitting below us."

And the other raven said, "*Poor* Claus, did you say, brother? Do you not see the witch-hazel lying on the ground beside him?"

The one raven said, "Oh yes; I see that, but what good does it do him?"

And the other raven said, "It does him no good now, but if he were to go home again and strike on the great stone on the top of the hill back of Herr Axel's house, then it would do him good; for in it lies a great treasure of silver and gold."

Claus had picked up his ears at all this talk, you may be sure. "See," said he, "that is the way that a man will pass by a great fortune in the little world at home to seek for a little fortune in the great world abroad"–which was all very true. After that he lost no time in getting back home again.

"What! are you back again?" said Hans.

"Oh yes," said Claus, "I am back again."

"That is always the way with a pewter penny," said Hans—for that is how some of us are welcomed home after we have been away.

As for Claus, he was as full of thoughts as an egg is of meat, but he said nothing of them to Hans. Off he went to the high hill back of Herr Axel's house, and there, sure enough, was the great stone at the very top of the hill.

Claus struck on the stone with his oaken staff, and it opened like the door of a beer vault, for all was blackness within. A flight of steps led down below, and down the steps Claus went. But when he had come to the bottom of the steps, he stared till his eyes were like great round saucers; for there stood sacks of gold and silver, piled up like bags of grain in the malt-house.

Claus and the Manikin "Claus and the Manikin"

At one end of the room was a great stone seat, and on the seat sat a little manikin smoking a pipe. As for the beard of the little man, it was as long as he was short, for it hung down so far that part of it touched the stone floor.

"How do you find yourself, Claus?" said the little manikin, calling Claus by his name.

"So good!" said Claus, taking off his hat to the other.

"And what would you like to have, Claus?" said the little man.

"I would like," said Claus, "to have some money, if you please."

"Take what you want," said the little man, "only do not forget to take the best with you."

Oh no; Claus would not forget the best; so he held the staff tighter than ever in his fist—for what could be better than the staff that brought him there? So he went here and there, filling his pockets with the gold and silver money till they bulged out like the pockets of a thief in the orchard; but all the time he kept tight hold of his staff, I can tell you.

When he had as much as his pockets could hold, he thanked the little manikin and went his way, and the stone door closed behind him.

And now Claus lived like a calf in the green corn-field. Everything he had was of the best, and he had twice as much of that as any of the neighbors. Then how brother Hans stared and scratched his head and wondered, when he saw how Claus sat in the sun all day, doing nothing but smoking his pipe and eating of the best, as though he were a born prince! Every day Claus went to the little man in the hill with his pockets empty, and came back with them stuffed with gold and silver money. At last he had so much that he could not count it, and so he had to send over to brother Hans for his quart-pot, so that he might measure it.

But Hans was cunning. "I will see what makes brother Claus so well-off in the world all of a sudden," said he; so he smeared the inside of the quart-pot with bird-lime.

Then Claus measured his gold and silver money in Hans's quart-pot, and when he was done with it he sent it back again. But more went back with the quart-pot than came with it, for two gold-pieces stuck to the birdlime, and it was these that went back with the pot to brother Hans.

Hans discovers Claus's Luck "Hans discovers Claus's Luck"

"What!" cried Hans, "has that stupid Claus found so much money that he has to measure it in a quart-pot? We must see the inside of this business!" So off he went to

Claus's house, and there he found Claus sitting in the sun and smoking his pipe, just as though he owned all of the world.

"Where did you get all that money, Claus?" said Hans.

Oh! Claus could not tell him that.

But Hans was bound to know all about it, so he begged and begged so prettily that at last Claus had to tell him everything. Then, of course, nothing would do but Hans must have a try with the hazel staff also.

Well, Claus made no words at that. He was a good-natured fellow, and surely there was enough for both. So the upshot of the matter was that Hans marched off with the hazel staff.

But Hans was no such simpleton as Claus; no, not he. Oh no, he would not take all that trouble for two poor pocketfuls of money. He would have a bagful; no, he would have *two* bagfuls. So he slung two meal sacks over his shoulder, and off he started for the hill back of Herr Axel's house.

When he came to the stone he knocked upon it, and it opened to him just as it had done for Claus. Down he went into the pit, and there sat the little old manikin, just as he had done from the very first.

"How do you find yourself, Hans?" said the little old manikin.

Oh, Hans found himself very well. Might he have some of the money that stood around the room in the sacks?

Yes, that he might; only remember to take the best away with him.

Prut! teach a dog to eat sausages. Hans would see that he took the best, trust him for that. So he filled the bags full of gold, and never touched the silver–for, surely, gold is better than anything else in the world, says Hans to himself. So, when he had filled his two bags with gold, and had shaken the pieces well down, he flung the one over one shoulder, and the other over the other, and then he had as much as he could carry. As for the staff of witch-hazel, he let it lie where it was, for he only had two hands and they were both full.

But Hans never got his two bags of gold away from the vault, for just as he was leaving–bang! came the stone together, and caught him as though he was a mouse in the door; and that was an end of him. That happened because he left the witch-hazel behind.

That was the way in which Claus came to lose his magic staff; but that did not matter much, for he had enough to live on and to spare. So he married the daughter of the Herr Baron (for he might marry whom he chose, now that he was rich), and after that he lived as happy as a fly on the warm chimney.

Now, *this* is so–it is better to take a little away at a time and carry your staff with you, than to take all at once and leave it behind.

This illustrated poem depicts the tailor with a wooden sword standing before the knight on horseback.

VENTURESOME BOLDNESS

A tailor came a-walking by,
The fire of courage in his eye.
"Where are you going Sir?" Said I.

"I slew a mouse
In our house
Where other tailors live," said he,
"And not a Jack
Among the pack
Would dare to do the like; pardie!
Therefore, I'm going out to try
If there be greater men that I;
Or in the land
As bold a hand
At wielding brand as I, you see!"
The tailor came a-limping by
With woful face and clothes awry
And all his courage gone to pie.
"I met a knight
In armor bright
And bade him stand and draw," said he;
"He straightaway did
As he was bid,
And treated me outrageously.
So I shall get me home again,
And probably shall there remain.
A little man.
Sir, always can
Be great with folk of less degree!"
H. Pyle

This is a full page illustrated poem depicting: the dame in a chair with the pig sitting on the floor in front of her, the pig dancing in full dress, the pig in full dress bowing to a person, and the pig in full dress on bent knee before the lady he loved.

SUPERFICIAL CULTURE

I'll tell of a certain old dame;
The same
Had a beautiful piggy, whose name
Was James;
and whose beauty and worth,
From the day of his birth,
Were matters of popular fame,
And his claim
To gentility no one could blame.
So, seeing his promise, she thought
She ought
To have him sufficiently taught
The art
Of deportment, to go
Into company; so

A master of dancing she brought,
Who was fraught
With a style which the piggiwig caught.
So his company manners were rare.
His care
Of social observances there
Would bear
The closest inspection,
And not a reflection
Could rest on his actions, howe'er
You might care
To examine 'em down to a hair.
Now, things went beau-ti-ful-ly,
Till he
Fell in love with a dame of degree;
Pardie!
When he tried for to speak,
But could only say, "O w-e-e-k!"
For, whatever his polish might be,
Why, dear me!
He was pig at the bottom, you see.
H. PYLE

HOW DAME MARGERY TWIST SAW MORE THAN WAS GOOD FOR HER

If one could always hold one's tongue as to what one sees, one would be the better for it. They are the wise people of this world who keep silence as to what they see; many such there are who behold things such as neither you nor I may ever hope to look upon, and yet we know nothing of this because they say nothing of it, going their own ways like common folks, and as though they saw nothing in an egg but the meat.

Dame Margery Twist of Tavistock town was not one of these wise folks who hold their tongues; she was a good, gossiping, chattering old soul, whose hen never hatched a chick but all of the neighbors knew of it, as the saying goes. The poor old creature had only one eye; how she lost the other you shall presently hear, and also how her wonderful tulip garden became like anybody else's tulip garden.

Dame Margery Twist lived all alone with a great tabby cat. She dwelt in a little cottage that stood back from the road, and just across the way from the butcher's shop. All within was as neat and as bright as a new pin, so that it was a delight just to look upon the row of blue dishes upon the dresser, the pewter pipkins as bright as silver, or the sanded floor, as clean as your mother's table. Over the cottage twined sweet woodbines, so that the air was ladened with their fragrance in the summer-time, when the busy, yellow-legged bees droned amid the blossoms from the two hives that stood along against the wall. But the wonder of the garden was the tulip bed, for there were no tulips in all England like them, and folks came from far and near, only to look upon them and to smell their fragrance. They stood in double rows, and were of all colors—white, yellow, red, purple, and pied. They bloomed early, and lasted later than any others, and, when they were in flower, all the air was filled with their perfume.

Now all of these things happened before the smoke of the factories and the rattling of the steam-cars had driven the fairy folks away from this world into No-man's-land, and this was the secret of the dame's fine tulip bed. For the fairies dwelt among the flowers, and she often told her gossips how that she could hear the fairy mothers singing their babies to sleep at night, when the moon was full and the evening was warm. She had never seen the little folks herself, for few folks are given to look upon them, and Dame Margery's eyes were not of that nature. Nevertheless, she heard them, and that, in my opinion, is the next best thing to seeing them.

Dame Margery Twist, as I said, was a good, kind, comfortable old soul, and was, moreover, the best nurse in all of Tavistock town. Was any one ill, it was Dame Margery who was called upon to attend him; as for the dame herself, she was always ready to bring a sick body into good health again, and was always paid well for the nursing.

DAME TWIST DRINKETH TEA "DAME TWIST DRINKETH TEA"

One evening the dame was drinking her tea by herself with great comfort. It was just at the dusking of the twilight; the latticed window was opened, so that the little breezes came rushing into the room, or stayed a while to play wantonly with the white linen curtains. The tabby cat was purring in the door-way, and the dame was enjoying the sweetness of the summer-time. There came a knock at the door, "Who is it?" said Dame Margery.

"It's Tommy Lamb, if you please, ma'am," said a little voice.

"Come in, Tommy," said the dame.

So in came Tommy Lamb, a little, curly-headed fellow, not any older than you, "What is it you want, Tommy?" said the dame.

"If you please, ma'am, there's a little gentleman outside, no taller than I be; he gave me this box, and told me to tell you to rub your eyes with the salve and then to come out to him."

The dame looked out of the window, but never a body stood there that she could see. "Where is the gentleman, dearie?" said she.

"Yonder he is, with a great white horse standing beside him," said Tommy Lamb, and he pointed with his finger as he spoke.

The dame rubbed her eyes and looked again, but never a thing did she see but the green gate, the lilac-bushes, and the butcher's shop opposite. The truth of the matter is, that little children like you, my dear, see things which we grown folks, with the dust of the world in our eyes, may never behold. "Well," said Dame Margery to herself, "this is strange, for sure! *I* see no little old gentleman in green." Then she opened the box that she held, and looked into it and saw that it was filled with a green salve. "I'll rub some of it on my eyes, at any rate," said she; whereupon she did so. Then she looked again, and, lo and behold! there stood a little old man, no taller than Tommy Lamb. His face was as brown, and as withered, and as wrinkled as a winter's crab-apple left on the bare tree when the frost is about. He was dressed all in green from top to toe, and on his head was a tall green cap, with a bell at the peak, which tinkled at every movement of his head. By his side stood a great, tall, milk-white horse, with a long tail and mane tied with party-colored ribbons.

THE LITTLE MAN AND THE GREAT HORSE "THE LITTLE MAN AND THE GREAT HORSE"

Dame Margery went out to the little old gentleman in green, and asked him what he would have with her. He told the dame that his wife was sorely sick, and that he wanted her to come and nurse her for the night. At this Dame Margery hemmed and hawed and shook her head, for she did not like the thought of going out at night, she knew not where, and with such a strange little body. Then the little man begged her and pleaded with her, and his voice and his words were as sweet as honey. At last he persuaded her to go, promising her a good reward if she would nurse his wife back into her health again. So the dame went back into the cottage to make ready for her journeying, throwing her red riding-cloak over her shoulders, and drawing her thick shoes upon her feet. Then she filled her reticule with a parcel of simples, in case they should be needed. After this she came out again, and climbed up behind the little man in green, and so settled herself upon the pillion saddle for her ride. Then the little man whistled to his horse, and away they went.

They seemed to fly rather than ride upon the hard ground, for the hedges and cottages and orchards flew past as though in a dream. But fast as they went, the old dame saw many things which she had never dreamed of before. She saw all of the hedge-rows, the by-ways, the woods and fields alive with fairy-folk. Each little body was busy upon his or her own business, laughing, chatting, talking, and running here and there like folks on a market-day.

DAME TWIST VISITS A STRANGE PATIENT "DAME TWIST VISITS A STRANGE PATIENT"

So they came at last to a place which the dame knew was the three-tree-hill; but it was not the three-tree-hill which she had seen in all of her life before, for a great gateway seemed to open into it and it was into this gateway that the little man in green urged the great white horse.

After they had entered the hill, Dame Margery climbed down from the pillion and stood looking about her. Then she saw that she was in a great hall, the walls of which were glistening with gold and silver, while bright stones gleamed like so many stars all over the roof of the place. Three little fairy children were playing with golden balls on the floor, and when they saw the dame they stopped in their sport and stood looking silently upon her with great, wide-opened eyes, just as though they were little mortal children. In the corner of the room was a bed all of pure gold, and over the bed were spread coverlets of gold and silver cloth, and in the bed lay a beautiful little lady, very white and ill. Then Dame Margery knew well enough that every one of these little people were fairies.

The dame nursed the fairy lady all that night, and by cock-crow in the morning the little woman had ease from her pain.

Then the little man spoke for the first time since Dame Margery had left home. "Look'ee, Dame Margery," said he; "I promised to pay you well and I will keep my word. Come hither!" So the dame went to him as he had bidden her to do, and the little man filled her reticule with black coals from the hearth. The dame said nothing, but she wondered much whether the little man called this good pay for her pains. After this she climbed up on the great horse again, and behind the little man, and they rode out of the place and home, where they were safe and sound ere the day had fairly broken. But before the little man had left her he drew out another little box just like the one that Tommy Lamb had brought her the evening before, only this time the box was filled with red ointment. "Rub your eyes with this, Dame Margery," said he.

DAME TWIST DRIVES AWAY THE LITTLE FOLKS "DAME TWIST DRIVES AWAY THE LITTLE FOLKS"

Now Dame Margery Twist knew butter from cheese, as the saying is. She knew that the green salve was of a kind which very few people have had rubbed over their eyes in this world; that it was of a kind which poets would give their ears to possess–even were it a lump no larger than a pea. So, when she took the box of red ointment, she only rubbed one eye with it–her left eye. Her right eye she pretended to rub, but, in truth, she never touched it at all.

Then the little man got upon his horse again, and rode away to his home in the hill.

After he had gone away, Dame Margery thought that she would empty her reticule of the dirty black coals; so she turned it topsy-turvy, and shook it over the hearth, and out tumbled–black coals? No; great lumps of pure gold that shone bright yellow, like fire, in the light of the candle. The good dame could scarcely believe her eyes, for here was wealth enough to keep her in comfort for all the rest of her days.

But Dame Margery's right eye! I wish I could only see what she saw with that right eye of hers! What was it she saw? That I will tell you.

The next night was full moon, and Dame Margery came and looked out over the fine bed of tulips, of which she was very proud. "Hey-day!" she cried, and rubbed her eyes, in doubt as to whether she was asleep or awake, for the whole place was alive with little folks.

But she was awake, and it was certain that she saw them. Yes; there they were–little men, little women, little children, and little babies, as thick in the tulip bed as folks at a wedding. The little men sat smoking their pipes and talking together; the little women sat nursing their babies, singing to them or rocking them to sleep in cradles of tulip flowers; the little children played at hide-and-seek among the flower-stalks. So the dame leaned out of the window, watching them with great delight, for it is always a delight to watch the little folks at their sports.

Dame Margery Twist goeth to see the merry doings at the Fair. "Dame Margery Twist goeth to see the merry doings at the Fair."

After a while she saw where one of the tiny fairy children hid himself under a leaf, while the others who were to seek him looked up and down, and high and low, but could find him nowhere. Then the old dame laughed and laughed to see how the others looked for the little fellow, but could not tell where he was. At last she could hold her peace no longer, but called out in a loud voice, "Look under the leaf, Blackcap!"

The words were no sooner out of her mouth than, whisk! whirr! off they scampered out of the garden and away–fathers, mothers, children, babies, all crying in their shrill voices, "She sees us! she sees us!" For fairies are very timid folk, and dread nothing more than to have mortals see them in their own shapes.

So they never came back again to the dame's garden, and from that day to this her tulips have been like everybody else's tulips. Moreover, whenever she went out the fairies scampered away before her like so many mice, for they all knew that she could see them with her magical eye. This, as you may see, was bad enough, but no other harm would have come of it if she had only gathered wisdom at that time, seeing what ill came of her speech. But, like many other old dames that I wot of, no sound was so pleasant to her ears as the words of her own mouth.

Now, about a twelvemonth after the time that the dame had nursed the fairy lady, the great fair was held at Tavistock. All the world and his wife were there, so, of course, Dame Margery went also. And the fair was well worth going to, I can tell you! Booths stood along in a row in the yellow sunlight of the summer-time, and flags and streamers of many colors fluttered in the breeze from long poles at the end of each booth. Ale flowed like water, and dancing was going on on the green, for Peter Weeks the piper was there, and his pipes were with him. It was a fine sight to see all of the youths and maids, decked in fine ribbons of pink and blue, dancing hand-in-hand to his piping. In the great tent the country people had spread out their goods–butter, cheese, eggs, honey, and the like–making as goodly a show as you would want to see. Dame Margery was in her glory, for she had people to gossip with everywhere; so she went hither and thither, and at last into the great tent where these things of which I have spoken were all spread out for show.

Dame Twist sees the little man in green for the last time "Dame Twist sees the little man in green for the last time"

Then, lo and behold! who should she see, gliding here and there among the crowd of other people, but the little man in green whom she had seen a year ago. She opened her eyes mightily wide, for she saw that he was doing a strange thing. By his side hung a little earthenware pot, and in his hand he held a little wooden scraper, which he passed over the rolls of butter, afterwards putting that which he scraped from the rolls into the pot that hung beside him. Dame Margery peeped into the pot, and saw that it was half full; then she could contain herself no longer.

"Hey-day, neighbor!" cried she, "here be pretty doings, truly! Out upon thee, to go scraping good luck and full measure off of other folks' butter!"

When the little man in green heard the dame speak to him, he was so amazed that he nearly dropped his wooden scraper. "Why, Dame Margery! can you see me then?"

"Aye, marry can I! And what you are about doing also; out upon you, say I!"

"And did you not rub your eyes with the red salve then?" said the little man.

"One eye, yes, but one eye, no," said the dame, slyly.

"Which eye do you see me with?" said he.

"With this eye, gossip, and very clearly, I would have you know," and she pointed to her right eye.

Then the little man swelled out his cheeks until they were like two little brown dumplings. Puff! he blew a breath into the good dame's eye. Puff! he blew, and if the dame's eye had been a candle, the light of it could not have gone out sooner.

The dame felt no smart, but she might wink and wink, and wink again, but she would never wink sight into the eye upon which the little man had blown his breath, for it was blind as the stone wall back of the mill, where Tom the tinker kissed the miller's daughter.

Dame Margery Twist never greatly missed the sight of that eye; but all the same, I would give both of mine for it.

All of these things are told at Tavistock town even to this day; and if you go thither, you may hear them for yourself.

But I say again, as I said at first: if one could
only hold one's tongue as to what one sees,
one would be the better for it.

This is a full page illustrated poem depicting: the three old maids gossiping at a table, the two old maids gossiping as the other leaves, and the last old maid sitting alone.

YE SONG OF YE GOSSIPS

1
One old maid,
And another old maid,
And another old maid–that's three–
    And they were agossiping, I am afraid,
As they sat sipping their tea.

2
They talked of this,
And they talked of that,
In the usual gossiping way
Until everybody was black as your hat,
And the only ones white were they.

3
One old maid,
And another old maid,–
For the third had gone into the street–
Who talked in a way of that third old maid,
Which never would do to repeat.

4
And now but one
Dame sat all alone,
For the others were both away.
"I've never yet met," said she, with a groan,
"Such scandalous talkers as they."

5
"Alas! and alack!"
"We're all of a pack!
For no matter how we walk,
Or what folk say to our face, our back
Is sure to breed gossip and talk."
H. PYLE

This is a full page illustrated poem depicting the two physicians walking, the two finding the crow, and the crow feet up on the path as they continue to argue.

A VICTIM TO SCIENCE

Th're were two wise physicians once, of glory and renown,
Who went to take a little walk nigh famous Concord town.

Oh! very, very great and wise and learned men were they,
And wise and learned was th'r talk, as they walked on th'r way.
And as they walked and talked and talked, they came to wh're they found
A Crow as black as any hat, a-sitting on ye ground.
Ye Crow was very, very sick, as you may quickly see
By just looking at ye picture th't is drawn h're by me.
Now wh'n ye doctors came to him they mended of th'r pace,
And said one unto ye other, "H're's an interesting case,
A case th't sh'ld be treated, and be treated speedily.
I have—yes, here it is—a pill th't has been made by me.
Now, I have had occasion—" Said ye other, "In most cases
Your pills are excellently good, but h're, my friend, are traces
Of a lassitude, a languor, th't your pills c'ld hardly aid;
In short, they're rather violent for th's, I am afraid.
I have a tincture—" Said ye first, "Your tincture cannot touch
A case as difficult as th's, my pills are better much."
"Your pills, sir, are too violent." "Your tonic is too weak."
"As I have said, sir, in th's case—" "Permit me, sir, to speak."
And so they argued long and high, and on, and on, and on,
Until they lost their tempers, and an hour or more had gone.
But long before their arguments ye question did decide,
Ye Crow, not waiting for ye end, incontinently died.
YE MORAL
(*is apparent.*)
H. Pyle

This is a full page illustrated poem depicting the wind in fairy form first playing with the tree and then as a tempest.

PLAY EARNEST
Over dewy hill and lea
Merrily
Rushed a mad-cap breeze at play,
And the daisies, like the bright
Stars at night,
Danced and twinkled in its way.
Now, a tree called to the breeze,
"Little breeze,
Will you come and have a play?"
And the wind upon its way
Stopped to play.
Then the leaves, with sudden shiver,
Sudden quiver,
Met the light
Mad-cap breeze
With delight.
Presently the breeze grew stronger,

For it cared to play no longer.
So it flung the limbs about,
And it tossed the leaves in rout,
Till it roared, as though with thunder.
Then the poor tree groaned and bent,
And the breeze,–a tempest,–rent
Leaves and branches from its crowns
Till, at last, it flung it down,
Stripped, and bare, and torn asunder.
H. Pyle

This is a full page illustrated poem with pictures of: "Ye King" praying, "Ye Saint" holding the baby with stork standing by, "Ye Stork" with baby in flight, and "Ye Cobbler" at work.

THE ACCIDENT OF BIRTH.

Saint Nicholas used to send, so I am told,
All new-born babes by storks, in days of old.

1

King Friedrich Max of Stultzenmannenkim,
For many years unto the Saint did pray,
That he would send unto his Queen and him,
A baby boy, to be the King some day.
At last the Saint the King's petition heard,
And called to him a sober long-legged bird.

2

Quoth he, "Good Wilhelm Stork (such was its name),
Here is a baby boy to take away.
It is for Fritz; so bear him to the same,
Or rather to his Queen, without delay.
For one grows weary when one always hears
The same words daily dinning in one's ears."

3

Now Wilhelm Stork was old, and dull of wits,
For age not always sharpens wisdom much,
So what does he but bear the gift to Fritz
The cobbler, who had half a score of such.
And so the baby, through a blunder, passed
From being first of all, unto–*ye last*.

4

From this I gather that a new-born Prince,
From new-born cobbler's somewhat hard to know,
For which of us could tell the difference, since
One thus experienced was mistaken so?
Also, perhaps, *I* should be great, instead
Of writing thus, to earn my daily bread.
H.P. MDCCCLXXXIII

CLEVER PETER THE TWO BOTTLES

"Yes, Peter is clever." So said his mother; but then every goose thinks her own gosling a swan.

The minister and all of the people of the village said Peter was but a dull block. Maybe Peter *was* a fool; but, as the old saying goes, never a fool tumbles out of the tree but he lights on his toes. So now you shall hear how that Peter sold his two baskets of eggs for more than you or I could do, wise as we be.

"Peter," said his mother.

"Yes," said Peter, for he was well brought up, and always answered when he was spoken to.

"My dear little child, thou art wise, though so young now; how shall we get money to pay our rent?"

"Sell the eggs that the speckled hen has laid," said Peter.

"But when we have spent the money for them, what then?"

"Sell more eggs," said Peter, for he had an answer for everything.

"But when the speckled hen lays no more eggs, what shall we do then?"

"We shall see," said Peter.

"Now indeed art thou wise," said his mother, "and I take thy meaning; it is this, when we have spent all, we must do as the little birds do, and trust in the good Heaven." Peter meant nothing of the kind, but then folks will think that such wise fellows as Peter and I mean more than we say, whence comes our wisdom.

So the next day Peter started off to the town, with the basket full of nice white eggs. The day was bright and warm and fair; the wind blew softly, and the wheatfields lay like green velvet in the sun. The flowers were sprinkled all over the grass, and the bees kicked up their yellow legs as they tilted into them. The garlic stuck up stout spikes into the air, and the young radishes were green and lusty. The brown bird in the tree sang, "Cuckoo! cuckoo!" and Peter trudged contentedly along, kicking up little clouds of dust at every footstep, whistling merrily and staring up into the bright sky, where the white clouds hung like little sheep, feeding on the wide blue field. "If those clouds were sheep, and the sheep were mine, then I would be a great man and very proud," said Peter. But the clouds were clouds, and he was not a great man; nevertheless, he whistled more merrily than ever, for it was very nice to think of these things.

So he trudged along with great comfort until high noontide, against which time he had come nigh to the town, for he could see the red roofs and the tall spires peeping over the crest of the next green hill. By this time his stomach was crying, "Give! give!" for it longed for bread and cheese. Now, a great gray stone stood near by at the forking of the road, and just as Peter came to it he heard a noise. "Click! clack!" he turned his head, and, lo and behold! the side of the stone opened like a door, and out came a little old man dressed all in fine black velvet. "Good-day, Peter," said he. "Good-day, sir," said Peter, and he took off his hat as he spoke, for he could see with half an eye that this little old gentleman was none of your cheese-paring fine folks.

"Will you strike a bargain with me for your eggs?" said the little old man. Yes, Peter would strike a bargain; what would the little gentleman give him for his eggs?

"I will give you this," said the little old man, and he drew a black bottle out of his pocket.

Peter took the bottle and turned it over and over in his hands. "It is," said he, "a pretty little, good little, sweet little bottle, but it is not worth as much as my basket of eggs."

"Prut!" said the little gentleman, "now you are not talking like the wise Peter. You should never judge by the outside of things. What would you like to have?"

"I should like," said Peter, "to have a good dinner."

"Nothing easier!" said the little gentleman, and he drew the cork. Pop! pop! and what should come out of the bottle but two tall men, dressed all in blue with gold trimmings. "What will you have, sir?" said the first of these to the little gentleman.

"A good dinner for two," said the little man.

No sooner said than done; for, before you could say Frederic Strutzenwillenbachen, there stood a table, with a sweet, clean, white cloth spread over it, and on this was the nicest dinner that you ever saw, for there were beer and chitterlings, and cheese and good white bread, fit for the king. Then Peter and the little man fell to with might and main, and ate till they could eat no more. After they were done, the two tall men took table and dishes and all back into the bottle again, and the little gentleman corked it up.

Clever Peter the Little Gentleman in Black "Clever Peter the Little Gentleman in Black"

"Yes," said Peter, "I will give you my basket of eggs for the little black bottle." And so the bargain was struck. Then Peter started off home, and the little man went back again into the great stone and closed the door behind him. He took the basket of eggs with him; where he took it neither Peter nor I will ever be able to tell you.

So Peter trudged along homeward, until, after a while, the day waxing warm, he grew tired. "I wish," said he, "that I had a fine white horse to ride."

Then he took the cork out of the bottle. Pop! pop! and out came the two tall fellows, just as they had done for the little old man. "What will you have, sir?" said the first of them.

"I will have," said Peter, "a fine white horse to ride."

No sooner said than done; for there, before him in the road, stood a fine white horse, with a long mane and tail, just like so much spun silk. In his mouth was a silver bit; on his back was a splendid saddle, covered all over with gold and jewels; on his feet were shoes of pure gold, so that he was a very handsome horse indeed.

Peter mounted on his great horse and rode away home, as grand as though he were a lord or a nobleman.

Every one whom he met stopped in the middle of the road and looked after him. "Just look at Peter!" cried they; but Peter held his chin very high, and rode along without looking at them, for he knew what a fine sight he was on his white horse.

And so he came home again.

"What didst thou get for thy eggs, my little duck?" said his mother.

"I got a bottle, mother," said Peter.

Then at first Peter's mother began to think as others thought, that Peter was a dull block. But when she saw what a wonderful bottle it was, and how it held many good things and one over, she changed her mind again, and thought that her Peter was as wise as the moon.

And now nothing was lacking in the cottage; if Peter and his mother wanted this, it came to them; if they wished for that, the two tall men in the bottle fetched it. They lined the house all inside with pure gold, and built the chimneys of bricks of silver, so that there was nothing so fine between all the four great rivers. Peter dressed in satin and his mother in silk, and everybody called him "Lord Peter." Even the minister of the village said that he was no dull boy, for nobody is dull who rides on horseback and never wears wooden shoes. So now Peter was a rich man.

Clever Peter rides to the King's Palace upon his fine Horse "Clever Peter rides to the King's Palace upon his fine Horse"

One morning Peter said to his mother, "Mother, I am going to ask the King to let me marry his daughter."

To this his mother said nothing, for surely her Peter was as good as any princess that ever lived.

So off Peter rode, dressed all in his best and seated astride of a grand horse. At last he came to the palace which was finer than the handsome new house of Herr Mayor Kopff. Rap! rap! rap! Peter knocked at the door, and presently came a neat servant girl and opened it to him. "Is the King at home, my dear?" said Peter.

Yes, the King was at home; would he come into the parlor and sit down? So Peter went into the parlor and sat down, and then the King came in, dressed all in his best dressing-gown, with silver slippers upon his feet, and a golden crown upon his head.

"What is your name?" said the King.

"Peter Stultzenmilchen," said Peter.

"And what do you want, Lord Peter," said the King; for, as I have said, Peter was dressed in his best clothes, and the old King thought that he was a great lord.

"I want to marry your daughter," said Peter.

To this the King said "Hum-m-m," and Peter said nothing. Then the King said that he had determined that no one should marry his daughter without bringing him a basketful of diamonds, rubies, topazes, emeralds, pearls, and all manner of precious stones; for he thought by this to get rid of Peter.

"Is that all?" said Peter. "Nothing is easier."

So off he went, until he came to a chestnut woods just back of the royal kitchen-garden. There he uncorked his bottle. Pop! pop! and out came the two tall men. "What will you have, sir?" said they. Peter told them what he wanted, and it was no sooner said than done; for, there on the ground before him, stood a basketful of all kinds of precious stones; each of them was as large as a hen's egg, and over all of them was spread a nice clean white napkin. So Peter took the basket on his arm and went back again to the palace.

But how the King did open his eyes, to be sure, and how he stared! "Now," said Peter, "I should like to marry your daughter, if you please."

At this the King hemmed and hawed again. No, Peter could not marry the Princess yet, for the King had determined that no man should marry his daughter without bringing him a bird all of pure silver that could sing whenever it was wanted, and that more sweetly than a nightingale; for he thought that now he should be rid of Peter, at any rate.

"Nothing easier," said Peter, and off he went again.

When he had come to the chestnut woods, he uncorked his bottle and told the two tall men what he wanted. No sooner said than done; for there was a bird all of pure silver. And not only that, but the bird sat in a little golden tree, and the leaves of the tree were emeralds, and rubies hung like cherries from the branches.

Then Peter wrapped this up in his handkerchief and took it to the palace. As for the King, he could not look at it or listen to it enough.

"Now," said Peter, "I should like to marry your daughter, if you please."

But at this the King sang the same tune again. No, Peter could not marry his daughter yet, for the King had determined that the man who was to marry his daughter should first bring him a golden sword, so keen that it could cut a feather floating in the air, yet so strong that it could cut through an iron bar.

"Nothing easier," said Peter, and this time the men of the bottle brought him such a sword as he asked for, and the hilt was studded all over with precious stones, so that it was very handsome indeed. Then Peter brought it to the King, and it did as the King would have it—it cut through a feather floating in the air; as for the iron bar, it cut through that as easily as you would bite through a radish.

Peter Eats With the King and Princess "Peter Eats With the King and Princess"

And now it seemed as though there was nothing else to be done but to let Peter marry the Princess. So the King asked him in to supper, and they all three sat down together, the King and the Princess and Peter. And it was a fine feast, I can tell you, for they had both white and red wine, besides sausages and cheese, and real white bread and puddings, and all manner of good things; for kings and princesses eat and drink of the best.

As for Peter, he made eyes at the Princess, and the Princess looked down on her plate and blushed, and Peter thought that he had never seen such a pretty girl.

After a while the King began to question Peter how he came by all these fine things—the precious stones, the silver bird, and the golden sword; but no, Peter would not tell. Then the King and the Princess begged and begged him, until, at last, Peter lost his wits and told all about the bottle. Then the King said nothing more, and presently, it being nine o'clock, Peter went to bed. After he had gone the King and the Princess put their heads together, and the end of the matter was that the wicked King went to Peter's room and stole the bottle from under the pillow where he had hidden it, and put one in its place that was as empty as a beer barrel after the soldiers have been in the town; for the King and the Princess thought that it would be a fine thing to have the bottle for themselves.

When the next morning had come, and they were all sitting at their breakfast together, the King said, "Now, Lord Peter, let us see what your bottle will do; give us such and such a kind of wine."

"Nothing easier," said Peter. Then he uncorked the bottle, but not so much as a single dead fly came out of it.

"But where is the wine?" said the King.

"I do not know," said Peter.

At this the King called him hard names and turned him out of the palace, neck and heels; so back poor Peter went to his mother with a flea in his ear, as the saying is. Now he was poor again, and everybody called him a dull block, for he rode no great white horse and he wore wooden shoes.

"Never mind," said his mother, "here is another basket of eggs from the speckled hen." So Peter set off with these to the market town, as he had done with the others before. When he had come to the great stone at the forking of the road, whom should he meet but the same little gentleman he had met the first time. "Will you strike a bargain?" said he. Yes, Peter would strike a bargain, and gladly. Thereupon the little old man brought out another black bottle.

"Two men are in this bottle," said the little old man; "when they have done all that you want them to do, say 'brikket-ligg' and they will go back again. Will you trade with me?" Yes, Peter would trade. So Peter gave the little man the eggs, and the little man gave Peter the second bottle, and they parted very good friends.

After a while Peter grew tired. "Now," said he to himself, "I will ride a little"; and so he drew the cork out of the bottle. Pop! pop! out came two men from the bottle; but this time they were ugly and black, and each held a stout stick in his hand. They said not a word, but, without more ado, fell upon Peter and began threshing him as though he was wheat on the barn floor. "Stop! stop!" cried Peter, and he went hopping and skipping up and down, and here and there, but it seemed as though the two ugly black men did not hear him, for the blows fell as thick as hail on the roof. At last he gathered his wits together, like a flock of pigeons, and cried, "Brikket-ligg! brikket-ligg!" Then, whisk! pop! they went back into the bottle again, and Peter corked it up, and corked it tightly, I can tell you.

Clever Peter and the Unlucky Bottle "Clever Peter and the Unlucky Bottle"

The next day he started off to the palace once more. Rap! rap! rap! he knocked at the door. Was the King at home? Yes, the King was at home; would he come and sit in the parlor?

Presently the King came in, in dressing-gown and slippers. "What! are you back again?" said he.

"Yes; I am back again," said Peter.

"What do you want?" said the King.

"I want to marry the Princess," said Peter.

"What have you brought this time?" said the King.

"I have brought another bottle," said Peter.

Then the King rubbed his hands and was very polite indeed, and asked Peter in to breakfast, and Peter went. So they all three sat down together, the King, the Princess, and Peter.

"My dear," said the King, to the Princess, "the Lord Peter has brought another bottle with him." Thereat the Princess was very polite also. Would Lord Peter let them see the bottle? Oh yes! Peter would do that: so he drew it out of his pocket and sat it upon the table.

Perhaps they would like to have it opened. Yes, that they would. So Peter opened the bottle.

Hui! what a hubbub there was! The King hopped about till his slippers flew off, his dressing-gown fluttered like great wings, and his crown rolled off from his head and across the floor, like a quoit at the fair. As for the Princess, she never danced in all of her life as she danced that morning. They made such a noise that the soldiers of the Royal Guard came running in; but the two tall black men spared them no more than the King and the Princess. Then came all of the Lords of the Council, and they likewise danced to the same music as the rest.

"Oh, Peter! dear Lord Peter! cork up your men again!" they all cried.

"Will you give me back my bottle?" said Peter.

"Yes! yes!" cried the King.

"Will you marry me?" said Peter.

"Yes! yes!" cried the Princess.

Then Peter said "brikket-ligg!" and the two tall men popped back into the bottle again. So the King gave him back his other bottle, and the minister was called in and married him to the Princess.

After that he lived happily, and when the old King died he became King over all of the land. As for the Princess, she was as good a wife as you ever saw, but Peter always kept the bottle near to him—maybe that was the reason.

Ah me! if I could only take my eggs to such a
market and get two such bottles for them!
What would I do with them? It would
take too long to tell you.

Clever Peter opens the Unlucky Bottle for the King and Princess "Clever Peter opens the Unlucky Bottle for the King and Princess"

This is a full page poem showing the three tailors walking together, the three approaching the milk-maids, and the three walking away saddened.

YE ROMANTIC ADVENTURES OF THREE TAILORS

Three little men went ajogging along–
Along in the sunshiny weather.
And they laughed and they sang an occasional song
Which they all of them caroled together.
And the great white clouds floated over the sky
And the day it was warm and the sun it was high.
As three jolly tailor men all were they
As you'd find in a dozen of years.
One carried the yardstick another the goose
And the bravest of all bore the shears
So they merrily trudged until after awhile
The came where three milk-maids sat all on a stile.
The grass it was green and the flowers were gay,
And it was the pleasantest weather.
And the milkmaids were pretty as blossoms in May
As they sat on the stile all together.
Then they stopped on the high-way those three gallant men
For they never had seen as fair lasses as then.

Then up spake the first of the tailor men three
And the one with the goodliest parts.
"We are all of us good men gallant and free
And have never yet plighted our hearts.
So prithee fair maids will you marry us all
For our hearts they be great as our bodies be small."
Then up spake the first of the three pretty dears
"Pray tell what your fortunes may be sir."
"Oh three loving hearts and a yard goose and shears."
"Then you've not enough fortune for me sir.
So get you along while your boots are still green
For richer young men we shall marry I ween."
Three little tailor men jogging along–
Along in the sunshiny weather.
No longer they laugh with a jest and a song
But they walk very sadly together.
For when maidens are proud like the milkmaidens cold,
The lads they grow sad like the tailors so bold.
Howard Pyle

This is an illustrated poem with the shepherd and shepherdess sitting in the grass above the poem, and the two of them sick with their heads wrapped on either side of the poem.

FANCY AND FACT

O! a shepherd and a shepherdess,
They dwelt in Arcadee,
And they were dressed in Watteau dress,
Most charming for to see.
They sat upon the dewy grass,
With buds and blossoms set.
And the shepherd played unto the lass,
Upon a flageolet.
It seemed to me as though it was
A very pleasant thing;
Particularly so because
The time of year was Spring.
But, O! the ground was damp, and so,
At least, I have been told,
The shepherd caught the lumbago,
The shepherdess, a cold.
My darling Child! the fact is
That the Poets often sing
Of those joys which in the practice
Are another sort of thing.
H.P.

This is a full page illustrated poem with the angel and faggot-maker sitting together, the faggot-maker going into the bottle, and the faggot-maker coming out again.

YE TWO WISHES

An Angel went a walking out one day, as I've heard said,
And, coming to a faggot-maker, begged a crust of bread
The faggot-maker gave a crust and something rather queer
To wash it down withall, from out a bottle that stood near.
The Angel finished eating; but before he left, said he,
"Thou shalt have two wishes granted, for that thou hast given me.
One wish for that good drinkable, another for the bread."
The he left the faggot-maker all amazed at what he'd said.
"I wonder," says the faggot-maker, after he had gone,
"I wonder if there's any truth in that same little song!"
So, turning this thing over in his mind, he cast around,
'Till he saw the empty bottle where it lay upon the ground.
"I wish," said he, just as a test, "if what he said is so,
Into that empty bottle, now, that I may straightway go"
No sooner said that done; for,–*Whisk!* into the flask he fell,
Where he found himself as tightly packed as chicken in the shell.
In vain he kicked and twisted, and in vain he howled with pain;
For, in spite of all his efforts, he could not get out again.
So, seeing how the matter stood, he had to wish once more.
When, out he slipped, as easily as he'd gone in before.
If we had two wishes, granted by an Angel thus,
We would not throw away the good so kindly given us.
For first we'd ask for wisdom, which, when we had in store,
I'm very doubtful if we'd care to ask for anymore.
Howard Pyle

This illustrated poem depicts the wise man asking all sorts of people.

A VERSE WITH A MORAL BUT NO NAME

A wise man once, of Haarlem town,
Went wandering up, and wandering down,
And ever the question asked:
"If all the world was paper,
And if all the sea was ink,
And if the trees were bread and cheese,
What would we do for drink?"
Then all the folk, both great and small,
Began to beat their brains,
But they could not answer him at all,
In spite of all their pains.
But still he wandered here and there,
This man of great renown,
And still he questioned everywhere,
The folk of Haarlem town:

"If all the world was paper,
And if all the sea was ink,
And if the trees were bread and cheese,
What would we do for drink?"
Full thin he grew, as, day by day,
He toiled with mental strain,
Until the wind blew him away,
And he ne'er was seen again.
And now methinks I hear you say,
"Was ere a man so foolish, pray,
Since first the world began?"
Oh, hush! I'll tell you secretly
Down East there dwells a man, and he
Is asking questions constantly,
That none can answer, that I see,
Yet he's a wise-wise man!
H. Pyle

HANS HECKLEMANN'S LUCK

Hans Hecklemann had no luck at all. Now and then we hear folks say that they have no luck, but they only mean that their luck is bad and that they are ashamed of it. Everybody but Hans Hecklemann had luck of some kind, either good or bad, and, what is more, everybody carries his luck about with him; some carry it in their pocket-books, some carry it in their hats, some carry it on their finger tips, and some carry it under their tongues–these are lawyers. Mine is at this moment sitting astride of my pen, though I can no more see it than though it was thin air; whether it is good or bad depends entirely as to how *you* look upon it.

But Hans Hecklemann had no luck at all. How he lost it nobody knows, but it is certain that it was clean gone from him.

He was as poor as charity, and yet his luck was not bad, for, poor as he was, he always had enough for his wife and his family and himself to eat. They all of them worked from dawn to nightfall, and yet his luck was not good, for he never laid one penny on top of the other, as the saying is. He had food enough to eat, and clothes enough to wear, so his luck was not indifferent. Now, as it was neither good, bad, nor indifferent, you see that it could have been no luck at all.

Hans Hecklemann's wife was named Catherine. One evening when Hans came into the cottage with just enough money to buy them all bread and not a cracked farthing to spare, Catherine spoke to him of this matter.

"Hans," said she, "you have no luck at all."

Hans Hecklemann, Catherine. "Hans Hecklemann, Catherine."

"No," said Hans, "I have not," which was the truth, as I have already told you.

"What are you going to do about it?" said Catherine.

"Nothing at all," said Hans.

"Doing nothing puts no cabbage into the pot," said Catherine.

"It takes none out," said Hans.

"See, Hans," said Catherine; "go to the old wise woman in the wood and talk to her about it; who knows but that she can tell you how and where you lost your luck?"

"If I should find my luck it might be bad and not good," said Hans.

"It is worth having a look at," said Catherine; "you can leave it where you find it if it does not please you."

"No," said Hans; "when a man finds his luck he has to take it, whether he likes it or no."

So Hans talked, but he had made up his mind to do as Catherine said, to go and see the old wise woman in the wood. He argued with her, but he only argued with her to let her know how little was her knowledge and how great was his. After he had clearly shown her how poor her advice was, he took it. Many other men are like Hans Hecklemann.

So, early the next morning, Hans jogged along to the old wise woman's cottage, while the day was sweet and fresh. The hedgerows were covered all over with white blossoms, as though it was with so much snow; the cuckoo was singing among the budding branches, and the little flowers were looking up everywhere with their bright faces. "Surely," said Hans to himself, "if I find my luck on this day, it must be good and not ill."

So he came to the little red cottage at the edge of the wood wherein lived the wise woman who knew many things and one. Hans scraped his feet on the stones until they were clean, and then he knocked at the door.

"Come in," said the old wise woman.

She was as strange an old woman as one could hope to see in a lifetime. Her nose bent down to meet her chin, and her chin bent up to reach her nose; her face was gray with great age, and her hair was as white as snow. She wore a long red cloak over her shoulders, and a great black cat sat on the back of her chair.

"What do you want, Son Hans?" said she.

"I want to find my luck, mother," said Hans.

"Where did you lose it, Son Hans?" said she.

"That I do not know, mother," said Hans.

Then the old wise woman said "Hum-m-m!" in a very thoughtful voice, and Hans said nothing at all.

After a while she spoke again. "Have you enough to eat?" said she.

"Oh yes!" said Hans.

"Have you enough to drink?" said she.

"Plenty of water, enough of milk, but no beer," said Hans.

"Have you enough clothes to cover you?" said she.

"Oh yes!" said Hans.

"Are you warm enough in winter?" said she.

"Oh yes!" said Hans.

"Then you had better leave well enough alone," said she, "for luck can give you nothing more."

"But it might put money into my pocket," said Hans.

"And it might take away the good things that you already have," said she.

"All the same, I should like to find it again," said Hans; "if I could only lay my hands on it I might make good out of it, even if it is bad."

"I doubt that," said the old wise woman. Neverthe less, she saw that Hans was set in his own way, and that he only talked stiffness into his stubbornness. So she arose from her chair with much groaning, for her joints were stiffened with age, and limping to a closet in the wall she brought a book thence. Then she ran her finger down one page and up another, until she had found that which she sought. When she had found it she spoke:

Hans Hecklemann goes to the cottage of the old Wise Woman in search of his Luck. "Hans Hecklemann goes to the cottage of the old Wise Woman in search of his Luck."

"Son Hans, you lost your luck three years ago when you were coming from the fair at Kneitlingen. You sat down on the overturned cross that lies where three roads meet, and it fell out of your pocket along with a silver shilling. Now, Hans, your luck was evil, therefore it stuck to the good sign, as all evil things of that kind must, like a fly to butter. Also, I tell you this: when an evil manikin such as this touches the sign of the good cross, he becomes visible to the eyes of everybody who chooses to look upon him. Therefore go to the stone cross and you will find your luck running this way and that, but never able to get away from it." So say ing, the old woman shut her book again. Then she arose from her chair and went once more to the closet in the wall. This time she took from it a little sack woven of black goat's hair. "When you have found your luck again, put it into this little bag," said she; "once in it, no evil imp will be able to get out again so long as you keep the strings tied. And now good-bye!"

Hans Hecklemann and the Old Wise-Woman "Hans Hecklemann and the Old Wise-Woman"

Then Hans slipped the little sack into his pocket, and set out for the overturned stone cross where the three roads meet. When he had come to the place, he looked here and there, and this way and that, but for a long time he could see nothing at all. At last, after much looking, he beheld a little black beetle running hither and thither on the stone. "I wonder," said Hans, "if this can be my luck."

So saying, he caught the little beetle betwixt his finger and thumb, but very carefully, for he could not tell whether or not it might bite him. The beetle stuck to the stone as though it had been glued there, but, at last, Hans pulled it away; then–lo! it was not a beetle that he held in his hand, but a little manikin about as long as your thumb and as black as ink. Hans Hecklemann was so frightened that he nearly dropped it, for it kicked and screeched and rolled its red eyes in a very ugly way as he held it. However, he popped it into the little sack and pulled the strings tight, and there it was, safe and sound.

That is what Hans Hecklemann's luck was like.

So Hans having his luck secure in the little sack began to bargain with it. "What will you do for me if I let you out?" said he.

"Nothing at all," snarled his luck.

"Very well," said Hans, "we will see about that."

So he carried it home with him, and threw sack and all into a nasty pot where Catherine cast the scrapings of the dishes–the fat and what not that she boiled down into soap now and then. There he left his luck to stay until the next day, and then he went to it again. "What will you do for me if I will let you out now?" said he.

"Nothing at all," snarled his luck.

"Very well," said Hans, "we will see about that." So he let him stay where he was for another day. And so the fiddle played; every day Hans Hecklemann went to his luck and asked it what it would give him if he would let it out, and every day his luck said nothing; and so a week or more passed.

Hans finds his Luck "Hans finds his Luck"

At last Hans's luck gave in.

"See, Hans," it said one morning; "if you will let me out of this nasty pickle I will give you a thousand thalers."

"Ah no!" said Hans. "Thalers are only thalers, as my good father used to say. They melt away like snow, and then nothing is left of them. I will trust no such luck as that!"

"I will give you two thousand thalers," said his luck.

Hans Hecklemann ploughs for Gold "Hans Hecklemann ploughs for Gold"

"Ah no!" said Hans; "two thousand thalers are only twice one thousand thalers. I will trust no such luck as that, either!"

"Then what will you take to let me out, Hans Hecklemann?" said his luck.

"Look," said Hans; "yonder stands my old plough. Now, if you will give me to find a golden noble at the end of every furrow that I strike with it I will let you out. If not–why, then, into the soap you go."

"Done!" said Hans's luck.

"Done!" said Hans.

Then he opened the mouth of the sack, and–puff! went his luck, like wind out of a bag, and–pop! it slipped into his breeches pocket.

He never saw it again with his mortal eyes, but it stayed near to him, I can tell you. "Ha! ha! ha!" it laughed in his pocket, "you have made an ill bargain, Hans, I can tell you!"

"Never mind," said Hans, "I am contented."

Hans Hecklemann did not tarry long in trying the new luck of his old plough, as you may easily guess. Off he went like the wind and borrowed Fritz Friedleburg's old gray horse. Then he fastened the horse to the plough and struck the first furrow. When he had come to the end of it–pop! up shot a golden noble, as though some one had spun it up from the ground with his finger and thumb. Hans picked it up, and looked at it and looked at it as though he would swallow it with his eyes. Then he seized the handle of the plough and struck another furrow–pop! up went another golden noble, and Hans gathered it as he had done the other one. So he went on all of that day, striking furrows and gathering golden nobles until all of his pockets were as full as they could hold. When it was too dark to see to plough any more he took Fritz Friedleburg's horse back home again, and then he went home himself.

All of his neighbors thought that he was crazy, for it was nothing but plough, plough, plough, morning and noon and night, spring and summer and autumn. Frost and darkness alone kept him from his labor. His stable was full of fine horses, and he worked them until they dropped in the furrows that he was always ploughing.

"Yes; Hans is crazy," they all said; but when Hans heard them talk in this way he only winked to himself and went on with his ploughing, for he felt that he knew this from that.

But ill luck danced in his pocket with the golden nobles, and from the day that he closed his bargain with it he was an unhappy man. He had no comfort of living, for it was nothing but work, work, work. He was up and away at his ploughing at the first dawn of day, and he never came home till night had fallen; so, though he ploughed golden nobles, he did not turn up happiness in the furrows along with them. After he had eaten his supper he would sit silently behind the stove, warming his fingers and thinking of some quicker way of doing his ploughing. For it seemed to him that the gold-pieces came in very slowly, and he blamed himself that he had not asked his luck to let him turn up three at a time instead of only one at the end of each furrow; so he had no comfort in his gathering wealth. As day followed day he grew thin and haggard and worn, but seven boxes of bright new gold-pieces lay hidden in the cellar, of which nobody knew but himself. He told no one how rich he was growing, and all of his neighbors wondered why he did not starve to death.

So you see the ill luck in his breeches pocket had the best of the bargain, after all.

After Hans had gone the way of all men, his heirs found the chests full of gold in the cellar, and therewith they bought fat lands and became noblemen and gentlemen; but that made Hans's luck none the better.

From all this I gather:

That few folks can turn ill luck into good luck.

That the best thing for one to do is to let well enough alone.

That one cannot get happiness as one does cabbages—with money.

That happiness is the only good luck, after all!

This illustrated poem depicts the Rajah in the various stages of the poem.

YE SONG OF YE RAJAH YE FLY

Great and rich beyond comparing
Was the Rajah Rhama Jaring,
As he went to take an airing
With his Court one summer day.
All were gay with green and yellow;
And a little darky fellow
Bore a monstrous fun umbrella,
For to shade him on the way.
Now a certain fly, unwitting
Of this grandeur, came a-flitting
To the Royal nose, and sitting
Twirled his legs upon the same.
Then the Rajah's eyes blazed fire
At the insult, and the ire
In his heart boiled high and higher.
Slap! he struck, but missed his aim.
Then all trembled at this passion,

For he spoke in furious fashion.
"Saw ye how yon fly did dash on
To our august nose!" he said.
"Now let all within our nation
Wage a war without cessation
War of b-lood, ex-ter-mi-nation,
Until every fly is dead!!!!"
Now the while this war was raging,
That the rajah was a-waging,
Things that should have been engaging
His attention went to pot.
So he came at last to begging,
Though the flies continued plaguing.
For it's not so easy pegging
Out vexation thus, I wot.
From this you may see what all have to expect,
Who, fighting small troubles, great duties neglect.
H. Pyle

This full page illustrated poem shows the mistress walking along with others watching, until she steps into a small pool and scares some geese aloft.

PRIDE IN DISTRESS

Mistress Polly Poppenjay
Went to take a walk one day.
On that morning she was dressed
In her very Sunday best;
Feathers, frills and ribbons gay,–
Proud was Mistress Poppenjay.
Mistress Polly Poppenjay
Spoke to no one on her way;
Passed acquaintances aside;
Held her head aloft with pride;
Did not see a puddle lay
In front of Mistress Poppenjay.
Mistress Polly Poppenjay
Harked to naught the folk could say.
Loud they cried, "Beware the puddle!"
Plump! She stepped into the middle.
And a pretty plight straightway
Was poor Mistress Poppenjay.
Mistress Polly Poppenjay;
From your pickle others may
Learn to curb their pride a little;–
Learn to exercise their wit, till
They are sure no puddles may

Lie in front, Miss Poppenjay.
Howard Pyle

This full page poem has the saint at the door of a thin man with empty purse, then at the door with the man well fed and full purse, and finally the saint alone scratching his head.

PROFESSION PRACTICE

Once, when Saint Swithin chanced to be
A-wandering in Hungary,
He, being hungered, cast around
To see if something might be found
To stay his stomach.
Near by stood
A little house, beside a wood,
Where dwelt a worthy man, but poor.
Thither he went, knocked at the door.
The good man came. Saint Swithin said,
"I prithee give a crust of bread
To ease my hunger."
"Brother," quoth
The good man, "I am sadly loath
To say" (here tears stood on his cheeks)
"I've had no bread for weeks and weeks,
Save what I've begged. Had I one bit,
I'd gladly give thee half of it."
"How," said the Saint, "can one so good
Go lacking of his daily food,
Go lacking means to aid the poor,
Yet weep to turn them from his door?
Here–take this purse. Mark what I say:
Thou'lt find within it every day
Two golden coins."
Years passed. Once more
Saint Swithin knocked upon the door.
The good man came. He'd grown fat
And lusty, like a well-fed cat.
Thereat the Saint was pleased. Quoth he,
"Give me a crust for charity."
"A crust, thou say'st? Hut, tut! How now?
Wouldst come a-begging here? I trow,
Thou lazy rascal, thou couldst find
Enough of work hadst thou a mind!
'Tis thine own fault if thou art poor.
Begone, sir!" *Bang!*–he shut the door.
Saint Swithin slowly scratched his head.
"Well, I *am*–humph!–just so," he said.

"How very different the fact is
'Twixt the profession and the practice!"

HP

This full page illustrated poem shows the man in the tub on the sea, dreaming of the roasted pig.

A TALE OF A TUB

1

You may bring to mind I've sung you a song,
Of a man of Haarlem town.
I'll sing of another,–'t will not take long–,
Of equally great renown.

2

"I've read," said he, "there's a land afar,
O'er the boundless rolling sea,
Where fat little pigs ready roasted are:
Now, that is the land for me.

3

Where tarts may be plucked from the wild tart tree,
And puddings like pumpkins grow,
Where candies, like pebbles, lie by the sea,–
Now, thither I'll straightway go."

4

Now, what do you think I've heard it said
Was his boat, his oar, his sail?
A tub, a spoon, and a handkerchief red,
For to breast both calm and gale.

5

So he sailed away, for a livelong day;
And the sun was warm and mild,
And the small waves laughed as they seemed to play,
And the sea-gulls clamored wild.

6

So he sailed away, for a livelong day;
Till the wind began to roar,
And the waves rose high, and, to briefly say,
He never was heard of more.

H. PYLE

FARMER GRIGG'S BOGGART

Did you ever hear of a boggart? No! Then I will tell you. A boggart is a small imp that lives in a man's house, unseen by any one, doing a little good and much harm. This imp was called a boggart in the old times, now we call such by other names–ill-temper, meanness, uncharitableness, and the like. Even now, they say, you may find a boggart in some houses. There is no placing reliance on a boggart; sometimes he may seem to be of service to his master, but there is no telling when he may do him an ill turn.

Rap! tap! tap! came a knock at the door.

The wind was piping Jack Frost's, for the time was winter, and it blew from the north. The snow lay all over the ground, like soft feathers, and the hay-ricks looked as though each one wore a dunce-cap, like the dull boy in Dame Week's school over by the green. The icicles hung down by the thatch, and the little birds crouched shivering in the bare and leafless hedge-rows.

But inside the farm-house all was warm and pleasant; the great logs snapped and crackled and roared in the wide chimney-place, throwing red light up and down the walls, so that the dark night only looked in through the latticed windows. Farmer Griggs sat warming his knees at the blaze, smoking his pipe in great comfort, while his crock of ale, with three roasted crab-apples bobbing about within it, warmed in the hot ashes beside the blazing logs, simmering pleasantly in the ruddy heat.

Farmer Georgie Griggs "Farmer Georgie Griggs"

Dame Griggs's spinning-wheel went humm-m-m! hum-m-m-m-m! like a whole hiveful of bees, the cat purred in the warmth, the dog basked in the blaze, and little red sparks danced about the dishes standing all along in a row on the dresser.

But, rap! tap! tap! came a knock at the door.

Then Farmer Griggs took his pipe from out his mouth. "Did'ee hear un, dame?" said he. "Zooks now, there be somebody outside the door."

"Well then, thou gert oaf, why don't 'ee let un in?" said Dame Griggs.

"Look'ee now," said Georgie Griggs to himself, "sure women be of quicker wits than men!" So he opened the door. Whoo! In rushed the wind, and the blaze of the logs made as though it would leap up the chimney for fear.

"Will you let me in out of the cold, Georgie Griggs?" piped a small voice. Farmer Griggs looked down and saw a little wight no taller than his knee standing in the snow on the door-step. His face was as brown as a berry, and he looked up at the farmer with great eyes as bright as those of a toad. The red light of the fire shone on him, and Georgie Griggs saw that his feet were bare and that he wore no coat.

"Who be 'ee, little man?" said Farmer Griggs.

"I'm a boggart, at your service."

"Na, na," said Farmer Griggs, "thee's at na sarvice o'mine. I'll give na room in my house to the likes o' thee"; and he made as though he would have shut the door in the face of the little urchin.

"But listen, Georgie Griggs," said the boggart; "I will do you a good service."

Then Farmer Griggs did listen. "What sarvice will'ee do me, then?" said he.

Dame Mally Griggs "Dame Mally Griggs"

"I'll tend your fires," said the manikin, "I'll bake your bread, I'll wash your dishes, I'll scour your pans, I'll scrub your floors, I'll brew your beer, I'll roast your meat, I'll boil your water, I'll stuff your sausages, I'll skim your milk, I'll make your butter, I'll press your cheese, I'll pluck your geese, I'll spin your thread, I'll knit your stockings, I'll mend your clothes, I'll patch your shoes–I'll be everywhere and do all of the work in your house, so that you will not have to give so much as a groat for wages to cook, scullion, or serving wench!"

Farmer Griggs and the Boggart. "Farmer Griggs and the Boggart."

Then Farmer Griggs listened a little longer without shutting the door, and so did Dame Griggs. "What's thy name, boggart?" said he.

"Hardfist," said the boggart; and he came a little farther in at the door, for he saw that Farmer Griggs had a mind to let him in all of the way.

"I don't know," said Georgie Griggs, scratching his head doubtfully; "it's an ill thing, lettin' mischief intull the house! Thee's better outside, I doubt."

"Shut the door, Georgie!" called out Dame Griggs; "thou'rt lettin' th' cold air intull th' room."

Then Farmer Griggs shut the door, but the boggart was on the inside.

This is the way in which the boggart came into Farmer Griggs's house, and there he was to stay, for it is no such easy matter getting rid of the likes of him when we once let him in, I can tell you.

The boggart came straightway over to the warm fire, and the dog growled–"chur-r-r-r!"–and showed his teeth, and the cat spit anger and jumped up on the dresser, with her back arched and her tail on end. But the boggart cared never a whit for this, but laid himself comfortably down among the warm ashes.

Now imps, like this boggart, can only be seen as the frost is seen–when it is cold. So as he grew warmer and warmer, he grew thin, like a jelly-fish, and at last, when he had become thoroughly warmed through, Farmer Griggs and the dame could see him no more than though he was thin air. But he was in the house, and he stayed there, I can tell you. For a time everything went as smooth as cream; all of the work of the house was done as though by magic, for the boggart did all that he had promised; he made the fires, he baked the bread, he washed the dishes, he scoured the pans, he scrubbed the floors, he brewed the beer, he roasted the meat, he stuffed the sausages, he skimmed the milk, he made the butter, he pressed the cheese, he plucked the geese, he spun the thread, he knit the stockings, he mended the clothes, he patched the shoes–he was everywhere and did all of the work of the house. When Farmer Griggs saw these things done, and so deftly, he rubbed his hands and chuckled to himself. He sent cook and scullion and serving maid a-packing, there being nothing for them to do, for, as I said, all of these things were done as smooth as cream. But after a time, and when the boggart's place had become easy to him, like an old shoe, mischief began to play the pipes and he began to show his pranks. The first thing that he did was to scrape the farmer's butter, so that it was light of weight, and all of the people of the market town hooted at him for giving less than he sold. Then he skimmed the children's milk, so that they had nothing but poor watery stuff to pour over their pottage of a morning. He took the milk from the cat, so that it was like to starve; he even pilfered the bones and scrapings of the dishes from the poor house-dog, as though he was a very magpie. He blew out the rush-lights, so that they were all in the dark after sunset; he made the fires burn cold, and played a hundred and forty other impish tricks of the like kind. As for the poor little children, they were always crying and complaining that the boggart did this and the boggart did that; that he scraped the butter from their bread and pulled the coverlids off of them at night.

Still the boggart did his work well, and so Farmer Griggs put up with his evil ways as long as he could. At last the time came when he could bear it no longer. "Look'ee, now, Mally," said he to his dame, "it's all along o' thee that this trouble's coome intull th' house. I'd never let the boggart in with my own good-will!" So spoke Farmer

Griggs, for even nowadays there are men here and there who will now and then lay their own bundle of faults on their wives' shoulders.

"I bade thee do naught but shut the door!" answered Dame Griggs.

"Ay; it's easy enough to shut the door after the trouble's come in!"

"Then turn it out again!"

"Turn un out! Odds bodkins, that's woman's wit! Dost'ee not see that there's no turnin' o' un out? Na, na; there's naught to do but to go out ourselves!"

Yes; there was nothing else to be done. Go they must, if they would be rid of the boggart. So one fine bright day in the blessed spring-time, they packed all of their belongings into a great wain, or cart, and set off to find a new home.

Oft they trudged, just as you see in the picture, the three little children seated high up in the wain, and the farmer and the dame plodding ahead.

THE DEPARTURE "THE DEPARTURE"

Farmer Griggs and the Wise Man. "Farmer Griggs and the Wise Man."

Now, as they came to the bottom of Shooter's Hill, whom should they meet but their good neighbor and gossip, Jerry Jinks. "So, Georgie," said he, "you're leavin' th' ould house at last?"

"High, Jerry," quoth Georgie. "We were forced tull it, neighbor, for that black boggart torments us so that there was no rest night or day for it. The poor bairns' stomachs are empty, and the good dame's nigh dead for it. So off we go, like th' field-fares in the autumn–we're flittin', we're flittin'!"

Now on the wain was a tall, upright churn; as soon as Georgie had ended his speech, the lid of the churn began to clipper-clapper, and who should speak out of it but the boggart himself. "Ay, Jerry!" said he, "we're a flittin', we're a flittin', man! Good-day to ye, neighbor, good-day to ye! Come and see us soon time!"

"High!" cried Georgie Griggs, "art thou there, thou black imp? Dang un! We'll all go back tull th' old house, for sure it's better to bear trouble there than in a new place."

So back they went again–boggart and all.

By this you may see, my dear, if you warm an imp by your fire, he will soon turn the whole house topsy-turvy. Likewise, one cannot get rid of a boggart by going from here to there, for it is sure to be in the cart with the household things.

But how did Georgie Griggs get rid of his boggart? That I will tell you.

He went to Father Grimes, the wise man, who lived on in a little house on the moor. "Father Grimes," said he, "how shall I get rid of my boggart?"

Then Father Grimes told him to take this and that, and to do thus and so with them, and see what followed. So Farmer Griggs went to Hugh the tailor's, and told him to make a pretty red coat and a neat pair of blue breeches. Then he went to William the hatter's, and bade him to make a nice little velvet cap with a bell at the top of it. Then he went to Thomas the shoemaker's, and bade him to make a fine little pair of shoes. So they all did as he told them, and after these things were made he took them home with him. He laid them on a warm spot on the hearth where the boggart used to come to sleep at night. Then he and his dame hid in the closet to see what would follow.

Presently came the boggart, whisking here and dancing there, though neither the farmer nor the dame could see him any more than though he had been a puff of wind.

"Heigh-ho!" cried the boggart, "these be fine things for sure." So saying, he tried the hat upon his head, and it fitted exactly. Then he tried the coat on his shoulders, and it fitted like wax. Then he tried the breeches on his legs, and they fitted as though they grew there. Then he tried the shoes on his feet, and there never was such a fit. So he was clad in all his new clothes from top to toe, whereupon he began dancing until he made the ashes on the hearth spin around with him as though they had gone mad, and, as he danced, he sang:

"Cap for the head, alas poor head!
Coat for the back, alas poor back!
Breeks for the legs, alas poor legs!
Shoen for the feet, alas poor feet!
If these be mine, mine cannot be
The house of honest man, Georgie!"

So he went singing and dancing, and skipping and leaping, out of the house and away. As for Georgie Griggs and his dame, they never heard a squeak from him afterwards.

Thus it was that Farmer Griggs got rid of his boggart. All I can say is, that if I could get rid of mine as easily (for I have one in my own house), I would make him a suit of clothes of the finest silks and satins, and would hang a bell of pure silver on the point of his cap. But, alackaday! there are no more wise men left to us, like good Father Grimes, to tell one an easy way to get rid of one's boggart.

The Boggart Rejoices "The Boggart Rejoices"

This illustrated page depicts the father seeing the man sing to his daughter, the father chasing them with a whip, and then the two flying away from his as birds.

YE STORY OF A BLUE CHINA PLATE.

There was a Cochin Chinaman,
Whose name it was Ah-Lee
And the same was just as fine a man
As you could wish to see,
For he was rich and strong,
And his queue was extra long,
    And he lived on rice and fish and chiccory.
Which he had a lovely daughter,
And her name was Mai-Ri-An,
And the youthful Wang who sought her
Hand was but a poor young man;
So her haughty father said,
"You shall never, never wed
Such a pauper as this penniless young man!"
So the daughter and her lover,
They eloped one summer day,
Which Ah-Lee he did discover,
And pursued without delay;
But the Goddess Loo, I've heard,
Changed each lover to a bird,

And from the bad Ah-Lee they flew away.
Ah me! Ah-Lee; the chance is,
That we all of us may know
Of unpleasant circumstances
We would like to stay, but oh!
The inevitable things
Will take unto them wings,
And will fly where we may never hope to go.
I would further like to state,
That the tale which I relate,
You can see on any plate
That was made in Cochin China years ago.

    This illustrated poem depicts the two woman fighting, people plugging their ears near the goose, and running away from the goat.

MORAL BLINDNESS

There was an old woman, as I've heard say,
Who owned but a single goose.
And the dame lived over toward Truxton way,
And the animal ran at loose.
It cackled up and it cackled down,
Disturbing the peace of all the town:
Gentle and simple, knight and clown,
From the dawn to the close of the day.
Another old woman, of not much note,
Lived over toward Truxton way,
Who owned a goat with a shaggy black coat,
As I've heard the neighbours say.
And it was the fear of one and all;
Butting the great, butting the small,–
No matter whom,–who happened to fall
In the way of this evil goat.
Said the first old woman, "This ugly goat
Should never thus run at loose."
Said the second, "I wish they'd cut the throat
Of that noisy cackling goose."
And so it happened when e'er that they
Would meet each other upon the way
They'd bicker and hicker the livelong day
In the key of a scolding note.
But all the neighbours, great and small,
Complained of both with grievous tone.
From which I gather that we all
See other's faults and not our own.
H. PYLE

This illustrated poem shows the people gazing upon the peacock, and later running away covering their ears.

OVERCONFIDENCE

A peacock sat on ye garden wall
(See picture here to ye right),
An ye folk came crowding-great and small
For it chanced that none in ye town at all
Had ever seen such a sight
If you'd have been there perhaps you'd have heard
Ye folk talk thus, as they looked at ye bird:
"O crickety!–Law!–
O jimmeny me!–
I never yet saw!–
Who ever did see
Such a beautiful sight in the world before,
Since ye animals marched from ye old ark door?
O! Look at ye spots
In his tail! And ye lots
Of green and of blue in his beautiful wings!
I'd give a new shilling to know if he sings!"
Ye peacock says, "Surely, they'll greatly rejoice
To hear but a touch of my delicate voice."
(*Sings.*)
"O dear! O dear!–
O stop it!–O do!–
We never did hear
Such a hullballoo!
'Tis worse than ye noise that ye carpenters make
When they sharpen their saws!–Now, for charity's sake,
Give over this squalling,
And catermawalling!"
Cried all ye good people who chanced to be near;
Each thrusting a finger-tip into each ear.
You see ye poor dunce had attempted to shine
In a way that was out of his natural line.
H. Pyle

This page has the poem on one side, with the lady gazing up into the tree with the robin, and the lady warm in a house and robin outside in the snow at the bottom of the page.

THE FORCE OF NEED

"Hey, Robin! ho, Robin!
Singing on the tree,
I will give you white bread,
If you will come to me."
"Oh! the little breeze is singing

To the nodding dairies white,
And the tender grass is springing,
And the sun is warm and bright;
And my little mate is waiting
In the budding hedge for me;
So, on the whole, I'll not accept
Your kindly courtesy."
"Hey, Robin! ho, Robin!
Now the north winds blow
Wherefore do you come here,
In the ice and snow?"
"The wind is raw, the flowers are dead,
The frost is on the thorn,
So I'll gladly take a crust of bread,
And come where it is warm."
Oh, Children! little Children!
Have *you* ever chanced to see
One beg for crust that sneered at crumb
In bright prosperity?

HP

THE BIRD IN THE LINDEN TREE

Once there was a prince, and his name was John. One day his father said to him, "See, John; I am growing old, and after a while the time will come when I must go the way of everybody else. Now I would like to see you married before I leave you."

"Very well," said the Prince, for he always answered the King in seemly fashion; "and who shall it be?"

"Why not the Princess of the White Mountain?" said the old King.

"Why not, indeed?" said the young Prince, "only she is too short."

"Why not the Princess of the Blue Mountain?" said the old King.

"Why not, indeed?" said the young Prince, "only she is too tall."

"Why not the Princess of the Red Mountain?" said the old King.

"Why not, indeed?" said the young Prince, "only she is too dark."

"Then whom will you have?" said the old King.

"That I do not know," said the young Prince, "only this: that her brow shall be as white as milk, and her cheeks shall be as red as blood, and her eyes shall be as blue as the skies, and her hair shall be like spun gold."

"Then go and find her!" said the old King, in a huff, for his temper was as short as chopped flax. "And don't come back again till you've found her!" he bawled after the Prince as he went out to the door.

So the Prince went out into the wide world to find such a maiden as he spoke of—whose brow was as white as milk, whose cheeks were as red as blood, whose eyes were as blue as the skies, and whose hair was like spun gold—and he would have to travel a long distance to find such a one nowadays, would he not?

So off he went, tramp! tramp! tramp! till his shoes were dusty and his clothes were gray. Nothing was in his wallet but a lump of brown bread and a cold sausage, for he had gone out into the world in haste, as many a one has done before and since his day.

So he went along, tramp! tramp! tramp! and by-and-by he came to a place where three roads met, and there sat an old woman.

"Hui! hui! but I am hungry!" said the old woman.

Now the Prince was a good-hearted fellow, so he said to the old woman, "It is little I have, but such as it is you are welcome to it." Thereupon he gave the old woman the lump of brown bread and the cold sausage that was in his wallet, and the old woman ate it up at a bite.

"Hui! hui! but I am cold!" said she.

"It is little that I have, but such as it is you are welcome to it," said the Prince, and he gave the old woman the dusty coat off his back. After that he had nothing more to give her.

Ye King, Prince John "Ye King, Prince John"

"One does not give something for nothing," said the old woman, so she began fumbling about in her pocket until she found an old rusty key. And the best part of the key was, that whenever one looked through the ring of it, one saw everything just as it really was and not as it seemed to be.

Who would not give his dinner and the coat off his back for such a key?

After that the Prince stepped out again, right foot foremost, tramp! tramp! tramp! until evening had come, and he felt as hungry as one is like to do when one goes without one's dinner. At last he came to a dark forest, and to a gray castle that stood just in the middle of it. This castle belonged to a great, ugly troll, though the Prince knew nothing of that.

"Now I shall have something to eat," said he, and he opened the door of the castle and went in.

Only one person was within, and that was a maiden; but she was as black from head to foot as Fritz the charcoal burner. The Prince had never seen the like of her in all of his life before, so he drew the rusty key out of his pocket and took a peep at her through the ring of it, to see what manner of body she really was.

Then he saw that she was no longer black and ugly, but as beautiful as a ripe apple; for her forehead was as white as milk, her cheeks were as red as blood, her eyes were as blue as the skies, and her hair was like spun gold. Moreover, any one could see with half an eye that she was a real princess, for she wore a gold crown on her head, such as real princesses are never without.

"You are the one whom I seek," said the Prince.

"Yes, I am the one you seek," said she.

"And how can I free you from your enchantment?" said he.

"If you will abide here three nights, and will bear all that shall happen to you without a word, then I shall be free," said she.

"Oh yes, I will do that," said the Prince.

After that the black Princess set a good supper before him, and the Prince ate like three men.

By-and-by there was a huge noise, and the door opened and in came an ugly troll with a head as big as a bucket. He rolled his great saucer eyes around till he saw the Prince where he sat beside the fire.

The Prince aids the Old Woman "The Prince aids the Old Woman"

"Black cats and spotted toads!" bellowed he, "what are you doing here?"

But to this the Prince answered never a word.

"We shall see whether or no there is sound in you!" roared the troll. Thereupon he caught the Prince by the hair and dragged him out into the middle of the room. Then he snatched up a great cudgel and began beating the Prince as though he were a sack of barley-flour; but the Prince said never a word. At last the troll had to give over beating him, for the morning had come and the troll was afraid the sun would catch him; and if that were to happen, he would swell up and burst with a great noise. "We shall see whether you will come again!" said he, and then he left the Prince lying on the floor more dead than alive; and if anybody was sore in all of the world, the Prince was that man.

After the troll had left the house, the black Princess came and wept over the Prince; and when her tears fell on him, pain and bruise left him, and he was as whole as ever. When he looked he saw that the black Princess's feet were as white as silver.

The next night the troll came again, and with him two others. "Black cats and spotted toads!" bellowed he, "are you here again?" Then he caught the Prince by the hair and dragged him out into the middle of the floor, and all three of the trolls fell upon the Prince and beat him with clubs, as though he had been a sack of barley-flour. But the Prince bore this too without a word. At last the morning came, and they had to give over beating him. "We shall see if you will come again," said the troll of the house.

After the trolls had gone, the black Princess came and wept over the Prince as she had done before, and when her tears fell on him he was made whole again. And now the hands of the black Princess were as white as silver.

THE GREAT UGLY TROLL FINDS THE PRINCE BY THE FIRE "THE GREAT UGLY TROLL FINDS THE PRINCE BY THE FIRE"

The third night the troll of the house came, and brought with him six others. Then the same thing happened as before, and they beat the Prince with great cudgels as thick as my thumb. At last the morning came, and they went away bellowing and howling, for their enchantment had gone. As for the Prince, he lay upon the floor more dead than alive, for he could neither see nor hear anything that happened about him.

Then the Princess came for the third time and wept over him, and he was whole and sound again. As for the Princess, she stood before him, and now her brow was as white as milk, and her cheeks were as red as blood, and her eyes were as blue as the skies, and her hair was like spun gold. But the beautiful Princess had little or nothing upon her, so the Prince wrapped her in a ram's skin that was in the troll's house. Then he turned his toes the way he had come, and started away for home, taking her along with him.

So they went along and along till they had come so near to the King's house that they could see the high roofs and the weathercocks over the crest of the next hill. There the Prince bade the Princess to wait for him till he went home and brought her a dress of real silver and gold, such as was fitting for her to wear. Then he left her, and the Princess sat down beside the roadside to wait until he should come again.

Now as the Princess sat there, there came along the old goose-herd of the palace, and with her came her daughter; for they were driving the royal geese home again from where they had been eating grass. When they saw the beautiful Princess, clad in her ram's hide, they stared as though they would never shut their eyes again. Then they wanted to know all about her–who she was, and where she came from, and what she sat there for. So the Princess told them all that they wanted to know, and that she waited there for the Prince to come with a dress all of silver and gold, which would suit her better than the old ram's hide which she wore.

Then the old goose-woman thought that it would be a fine thing to have her daughter in the Princess's place, so that she might have the dress of real silver and gold, and marry the Prince. So the goose-herd's daughter held the Princess, and the old goose-herd stripped the ram's hide off from her.

No sooner had they done this than the Princess was changed into a beautiful golden bird, and flew away over hill and over valley. Then the goose-herd's daughter clad herself in the ram's hide, and sat down in the Princess's place.

The Gooseherd her Daughter meet the Princess at the Roadside "The Gooseherd her Daughter meet the Princess at the Roadside"

"Yes, my pretty little bird," said the old goose-herd, "thou wilt make a fine Princess!" But, prut! she was no more like a Princess than I am, for she was squat, and round-shouldered, and had hair of the color of tow.

Then the old goose-herd drove her geese away, and the goose-girl waited for the coming of the Prince.

Sure enough, after a while the Prince came with a fine dress, all of real silver and gold; but when he saw the goose-girl he beat his head with his knuckles, for he thought that it was the Princess, and that she was enchanted again.

Why did he not look through the ring of his magic key?

Perhaps for this, perhaps for that–one cannot be always wise.

The Prince looks through the Magic Key. "The Prince looks through the Magic Key."

Then the Prince dressed the goose-girl in the fine dress of gold and silver, and took her home with him. Hui! how everybody stared and laughed when they saw what kind of a Princess it was that the Prince brought home with him! As for the poor old King, he rubbed his spectacles and looked and looked, for he thought that this was a strange sort of a wife for the Prince to make such a buzz about. However, he said nothing, for he thought to himself that perhaps she would grow prettier by-and-by.

So orders were given for a grand wedding on Thursday, and the old King asked all of the neighbors to come, and even those who lived at a distance, for this was to be a very grand wedding indeed.

But the old goose-herd told her daughter to mix a sleeping powder with the Prince's wine at supper, for, if the real Princess were to come at all, she would come that night. So the goose-girl did as she was told, and the Prince drank the sleeping powder with his wine, and knew nothing of it.

That night the golden bird came flying, and sat in the linden tree just outside of the Prince's chamber window. Then she clapped her wings and sang:

"I wept over you once,
I wept over you twice,
I wept over you three times.
In the ram's skin I waited,
And out of the ram's skin I flew.
Why are you sleeping,
Life of my life?"

But the Prince slept as sound as a dormouse, and when the dawn came and the cocks crew the golden bird was forced to fly away.

The next night the false Princess did as she had done before, and mixed a sleeping powder with the Prince's cup of wine.

That night the golden bird came again, and perched in the linden tree outside of the Prince's window, and sang:

"I wept over you once,
I wept over you twice,
I wept over you three times.
In the ram's skin I waited,
And out of the ram's skin I flew.
Why are you sleeping,
Life of my life?"

But once more the Prince slept through it all, and when morning had come the golden bird was forced to fly away.

Now it chanced that that night some of the folk of the King's household heard the bird singing, and they told the Prince all about it. So when the third night came, and the false Princess gave the Prince the cup of wine with the sleeping powder in it, he threw the wine over his shoulder, and never touched so much as a drop of it.

That night the bird came for the third time, and sang as it had done before.

But this time the Prince was not sleeping. He jumped out of his bed and ran to the window, and there he saw the bird, and its feathers shone like fire because they were of pure gold. Then he got his magic key and looked through the ring of it, and whom should he see but his own Princess sitting in the linden tree.

Then the Prince called to her, "What shall I do to set you free from this enchantment?"

"Throw your knife over me," said the Princess.

No sooner said than done. The Prince threw his knife over her, and there she stood in her own true shape. Then the Prince took her to the King, and when the King saw how pretty she was, he skipped and danced till his slippers flew about his ears.

The next morning the old King went to the false Princess, and said, "What should be done to one who would do thus and so?"

The Old King Rejoices at His New Daughter-in-Law. "The Old King Rejoices at His New Daughter-in-Law."

To this the false Princess answered, as bold as brass, "Such a one should be thrown into a pit full of toads and snakes."

"You have spoken for yourself," said the King; and he would have done just so to her had not the true Princess begged for her so that she was sent back again to tend the geese, for that was what she was fit for.

Then they had the grandest wedding that ever was seen in all of the world. Everybody was asked, and there was enough for all to eat as much as they chose, and to take a little something home to the children beside. If I had been there I would have brought you something.

What is the meaning of all this?

Listen, I will tell you something.

Once there was a man, and he winnowed a whole

peck of chaff, and got only three good solid grains from

it, and yet he was glad to have so much.

Would you winnow a whole peck of chaff for only

three good grains? No? Then you will never know

all that is meant by this story.

This illustrated poem has the two talking to each other by a road.

A DISAPPOINTMENT

He

"I prithee, tell me wh're you live?

Oh Maid, so sweet and rare!"

She

"I am ye miller's daughter, sir,

And live just over th're"

He

"Of all ye Maids I ever saw,

You are beyond compare."

She

"Oh; Thank you, sir! Oh; thank you, sir!

Your words are very fair."

He

"So I w'ld ask you something, now;

If I might only dare."

She

"Now, you may ask me wh't you please,

For anything I care."

He

"Then will you marry me? For we.

W'ld make a goodly pair."

She

"I thank you sir; your offer, it

Is most extremely rare.

But as I am already wed,

You'r late, sir, for ye Fair."

At th's ye Bachelor walked away,

And talked to himself of th' Lass so gay—

"Her hair is very decidedly red;
And her eyes have somewhat of a cast in her head;
And her feet are large, and her hands are coarse;
And, without I'm mistaken, her voice is hoarse.
'Tis a bargain of wh'ch I am very well rid;
I am glad, on ye whole, I escaped as I did."
Howard Pyle

The illustrations show small insets of the lamb dancing, the four wolves sitting and watching the lamb dance, and finally a group of lambs looking at its tail as the wolves run away.

YE SAD STORY CONCERNING ON INNOCENT LITTLE *LAMB* AND FOUR WICKED *WOLVES*

A little lamb was gamboling,
Upon a pleasant day,
And four grey wolves came shambling,
And stopped to see it play
In the sun.
Said the lamb, "Perhaps I may
Charm these creatures with my play,
And they'll let me go away,
When I've done."
The wolves, they sat asmiling at
The playful thing, to see
How exceedingly beguiling that
Its pretty play could be.
See it hop!
But its strength began to wane,
Though it gamboled on in pain,
Till it finally was fain,
For to stop.
Oh! then there was a munching,
Of that tender little thing,
And a crunching and a scrunching,
As you'ld munch a chicken wing.
No avail
Was its cunning, merry play
For the only thing, they say,
That was left of it that day,
Was its tail.
So with me; when I am done,
And the critics have begun,
All they'll leave me of my fun
'Ll be the tale.
H Pyle

THE APPLE OF CONTENTMENT

There was a woman once, and she had three daughters. The first daughter squinted with both eyes, yet the woman loved her as she loved salt, for she herself squinted with both eyes. The second daughter had one shoulder higher than the other, and eyebrows as black as soot in the chimney, yet the woman loved her as well as she loved the other, for she herself had black eyebrows and one shoulder higher than the other. The youngest daughter was as pretty as a ripe apple, and had hair as fine as silk and the color of pure gold, but the woman loved her not at all, for, as I have said, she herself was neither pretty, nor had she hair of the color of pure gold. Why all this was so, even Hans Pfifendrummel cannot tell, though he has read many books and one over.

The first sister and the second sister dressed in their Sunday clothes every day, and sat in the sun doing nothing, just as though they had been born ladies, both of them.

As for Christine–that was the name of the youngest girl–as for Christine, she dressed in nothing but rags, and had to drive the geese to the hills in the morning and home again in the evening, so that they might feed on the young grass all day and grow fat.

The first sister and the second sister had white bread (and butter beside) and as much fresh milk as they could drink; but Christine had to eat cheese-parings and bread-crusts, and had hardly enough of them to keep Goodman Hunger from whispering in her ear.

This was how the churn clacked in that house!

Well, one morning Christine started off to the hills with her flock of geese, and in her hands she carried her knitting, at which she worked to save time. So she went along the dusty road until, by-and-by, she came to a place where a bridge crossed the brook, and what should she see there but a little red cap, with a silver bell at the point of it, hanging from the alder branch. It was such a nice, pretty little red cap that Christine thought that she would take it home with her, for she had never seen the like of it in all of her life before.

So she put it in her pocket, and then off she went with her geese again. But she had hardly gone two-score of paces when she heard a voice calling her, "Christine! Christine!"

She looked, and who should she see but a queer little gray man, with a great head as big as a cabbage and little legs as thin as young radishes.

"What do you want?" said Christine, when the little man had come to where she was.

Oh, the little man only wanted his cap again, for without it he could not go back home into the hill–that was where he belonged.

But how did the cap come to be hanging from the bush? Yes, Christine would like to know that before she gave it back again.

The little man asks far his cap. "The little man asks far his cap."

Well, the little hill-man was fishing by the brook over yonder when a puff of wind blew his cap into the water, and he just hung it up to dry. That was all that there was about it; and now would Christine please give it to him?

Christine did not know how about that; perhaps she would and perhaps she would not. It was a nice, pretty little cap; what would the little underground man give her for it? that was the question.

Oh, the little man would give her five thalers for it, and gladly.

No; five thalers was not enough for such a pretty little cap–see, there was a silver bell hanging to it too.

Well, the little man did not want to be hard at a bargain; he would give her a hundred thalers for it.

No; Christine did not care for money. What else would he give for this nice, dear little cap?

"See, Christine," said the little man, "I will give you this for the cap"; and he showed her something in his hand that looked just like a bean, only it was as black as a lump of coal.

"Yes, good; but what is that?" said Christine.

"That," said the little man, "is a seed from the apple of contentment. Plant it, and from it will grow a tree, and from the tree an apple. Everybody in the world that sees the apple will long for it, but nobody in the world can pluck it but you. It will always be meat and drink to you when you are hungry, and warm clothes to your back when you are cold. Moreover, as soon as you pluck it from the tree, another as good will grow in its place. *Now*, will you give me my hat?"

Oh yes; Christine would give the little man his cap for such a seed as that, and gladly enough. So the little man gave Christine the seed, and Christine gave the little man his cap again. He put the cap on his head, and–puff!–away he was gone, as suddenly as the light of a candle when you blow it out.

So Christine took the seed home with her, and planted it before the window of her room. The next morning when she looked out of the window she beheld a beautiful tree, and on the tree hung an apple that shone in the sun as though it were pure gold. Then she went to the tree and plucked the apple as easily as though it were a gooseberry, and as soon as she had plucked it another as good grew in its place. Being hungry she ate it, and thought that she had never eaten anything as good, for it tasted like pancake with honey and milk.

Christine and the Apple "Christine and the Apple"

By-and-by the oldest sister came out of the house and looked around, but when she saw the beautiful tree with the golden apple hanging from it you can guess how she stared.

Presently she began to long and long for the apple as she had never longed for anything in her life. "I will just pluck it," said she, "and no one will be the wiser for it." But that was easier said than done. She reached and reached, but she might as well have reached for the moon; she climbed and climbed, but she might as well have climbed for the sun–for either one would have been as easy to get as that which she wanted. At last she had to give up trying for it, and her temper was none the sweeter for that, you may be sure.

Christine's Mother and Sisters wish for the Apple. "Christine's Mother and Sisters wish for the Apple."

After a while came the second sister, and when she saw the golden apple she wanted it just as much as the first had done. But to want and to get are very different things, as she soon found, for she was no more able to get it than the other had been.

Last of all came the mother, and she also strove to pluck the apple. But it was no use. She had no more luck of her trying than her daughters; all that the three could do was to stand under the tree and look at the apple, and wish for it and wish for it.

They are not the only ones who have done the like, with the apple of contentment hanging just above them.

As for Christine, she had nothing to do but to pluck an apple whenever she wanted it. Was she hungry? there was the apple hanging in the tree for her. Was she thirsty? there was the apple. Cold? there was the apple. So you see, she was the happiest girl betwixt all the seven hills that stand at the ends of the earth; for nobody in the world can have more than contentment, and that was what the apple brought her.

II

One day a king came riding along the road, and all of his people with him. He looked up and saw the apple hanging in the tree, and a great desire came upon him to have a taste of it. So he called one of the servants to him, and told him to go and ask whether it could be bought for a potful of gold.

So the servant went to the house, and knocked on the door–rap! tap! tap!

"What do you want?" said the mother of the three sisters, coming to the door.

Oh, nothing much; only a king was out there in the road, and wanted to know if she would sell the apple yonder for a potful of gold.

Yes, the woman would do that. Just pay her the pot of gold and he might go and pluck it and welcome.

So the servant gave her the pot of gold, and then he tried to pluck the apple. First he reached for it, and then he climbed for it, and then he shook the limb.

But it was no use for him to try; he could no more get it–well–than *I* could if I had been in his place.

At last the servant had to go back to the King. The apple was there, he said, and the woman had sold it, but try and try as he would he could no more get it than he could get the little stars in the sky.

Then the King told the steward to go and get it for him; but the steward, though he was a tall man and a strong man, could no more pluck the apple than the servant.

The King reaches for the Apple "The King reaches for the Apple"

So he had to go back to the King with an empty fist. No; he could not gather it, either.

Then the King himself went. He knew that he could pluck it–of course he could! Well, he tried and tried; but nothing came of his trying, and he had to ride away at last without, having had so much as a smell of the apple.

After the King came home, he talked and dreamed and thought of nothing but the apple; for the more he could not get it the more he wanted it–that is the way we are made in this world. At last he grew melancholy and sick for want of that which he could not get. Then he sent for one who was so wise that he had more in his head than ten men together. This wise man told him that the only one who could pluck the fruit of contentment for him was the one to whom the tree belonged. This was one of the daughters of the woman who had sold the apple to him for the pot of gold.

When the King heard this he was very glad; he had his horse saddled, and he and his court rode away, and so came at last to the cottage where Christine lived. There they found the mother and the elder sisters, for Christine was away on the hills with her geese.

The King took off his hat and made a fine bow.

The wise man at home had told him this and that; now to which one of her daughters did the apple-tree belong? so said the King.

"Oh, it is my oldest daughter who owns the tree," said the woman.

So, good! Then if the oldest daughter would pluck the apple for him he would take her home and marry her and make a queen of her. Only let her get it for him without delay.

Prut! that would never do. What! was the girl to climb the apple-tree before the King and all of the court? No! no! Let the King go home, and she would bring the apple to him all in good time; that was what the woman said.

Well, the King would do that, only let her make haste, for he wanted it very much indeed.

As soon as the King had gone, the woman and her daughters sent for the goose-girl to the hills. Then they told her that the King wanted the apple yonder, and that she must pluck it for her sister to take to him; if she did not do as they said they would throw her into the well. So Christine had to pluck the fruit; and as soon as she had done so the oldest sister wrapped it up in a napkin and set off with it to the King's house, as pleased as pleased could be. Rap! tap! tap! she knocked at the door. Had she brought the apple for the King?

Oh yes, she had brought it. Here it was, all wrapped up in a fine napkin.

The King talks with the Wise Man "The King talks with the Wise Man"

After that they did not let her stand outside the door till her toes were cold, I can tell you. As soon as she had come to the King she opened her napkin. Believe me or not as you please, all the same, I tell you that there was nothing in the napkin but a hard round stone. When the King saw only a stone he was so angry that he stamped like a rabbit and told them to put the girl out of the house. So they did, and she went home with a flea in her ear, I can tell you.

Then the King sent his steward to the house where Christine and her sisters lived.

He told the woman that he had come to find whether she had any other daughters.

The King's Steward and Christine "The King's Steward and Christine"

Yes; the woman had another daughter, and, to tell the truth, it was she who owned the tree. Just let the steward go home again and the girl would fetch the apple in a little while.

As soon as the steward had gone, they sent to the hills for Christine again. Look! she must pluck the apple for the second sister to take to the King; if she did not do that they would throw her into the well.

So Christine had to pluck it, and gave it to the second sister, who wrapped it up in a napkin and set off for the King's house. But she fared no better than the other, for, when she opened the napkin, there was nothing in it but a lump of mud. So they packed her home again with her apron to her eyes.

Christine gives the Apple to the King "Christine gives the Apple to the King"

After a while the King's steward came to the house again. Had the woman no other daughter than these two?

Well, yes, there was one, but she was a poor ragged thing, of no account, and fit for nothing in the world but to tend the geese.

Where was she?

Oh, she was up on the hills now tending her flock.

But could the steward see her?

Yes, he might see her, but she was nothing but a poor simpleton.

That was all very good, but the steward would like to see her, for that was what the King had sent him there for.

So there was nothing to do but to send to the hills for Christine.

After a while she came, and the steward asked her if she could pluck the apple yonder for the King.

Yes; Christine could do that easily enough. So she reached and picked it as though it had been nothing but a gooseberry on the bush. Then the steward took off his hat and made her a low bow in spite of her ragged dress, for he saw that she was the one for whom they had been looking all this time.

So Christine slipped the golden apple into her pocket, and then she and the steward set off to the King's house together.

When they had come there everybody began to titter and laugh behind the palms of their hands to see what a poor ragged goose-girl the steward had brought home with him. But for that the steward cared not a rap.

"Have you brought the apple?" said the King, as soon as Christine had come before him.

Yes; here it was; and Christine thrust her hand into her pocket and brought it forth. Then the King took a great bite of it, and as soon as he had done so he looked at Christine and thought that he had never seen such a pretty girl. As for her rags, he minded them no more than one minds the spots on a cherry; that was because he had eaten of the apple of contentment.

And were they married? Of course they were! and a grand wedding it was, I can tell you. It is a pity that you were not there; but though you were not, Christine's mother and sisters were, and, what is more, they danced with the others, though I believe they would rather have danced upon pins and needles.

"Never mind," said they; "we still have the apple of contentment at home, though we cannot taste of it." But no; they had nothing of the kind. The next morning it stood before the young Queen Christine's window, just as it had at her old home, for it belonged to her and to no one else in all of the world. That was lucky for the King, for he needed a taste of it now and then as much as anybody else, and no one could pluck it for him but Christine.

Now, that is all of this story. What does it mean? Can you not see? Prut! rub your spectacles and look again!

Manufactured By: RR Donnelley
                     Momence, IL USA
                     May, 2010